"Despite its importance, very few Christians would say they are satisfied with their prayer life. But instead of accepting that apathy, Daniel urges the reader to seek the face of the Lord in a way that will challenge and transform him. He lays out a practical and doable plan for Christians to take their prayer life from ordinary to extraordinary. Filled with personal stories and biblical examples, *Transforming Prayer* is a clear call for a more compelling prayer life."

—John MacArthur, Grace Community Church

"*Transforming Prayer* is a transforming message. Calling us out of self-involved, wish-list praying and into a passionate pursuit of the Present Jesus, Daniel Henderson has gifted the body of Christ with this treasure. A message distilled from his own journey, developed in his faithful ministry, and delivered with clarity and precision."

—Jennifer Kennedy Dean, The Praying Life Foundation

"As I work with pastors and counselors who serve multiplied thousands of believers all around the world, I am more convinced than ever about the desperate longing of the human heart to experience positive, permanent change. Nothing is more essential for this kind of transformation than the power of prayer. No one knows how to equip believers in prayer better than Daniel Henderson. I've experienced the relevance of his ministry and seen the impact of his teaching. I hope you will embrace the power of change available in this timely book."

—Tim Clinton, President, American Association of Christian Counselors

"When we change the way we pray, God changes the way we live. Unfortunately, many Christians get stuck in a rut of dry, dead praying that leaves them discouraged and confused. Daniel has spent his entire ministry equipping the church for a life of powerful prayer. I am confident the message of this book will awaken your heart and clarify a path to a new level of spiritual intimacy and transformation."

—Jonathan Falwell, Senior Pastor, Thomas Road Baptist Church

"*Transforming Prayer* is a well written, motivational, and a practical guide for us to pursue God together through worship-based prayer. Great movements of God are fueled by prayer, and this book is fuel for that fire. For those longing to see God move, this is a must-read."

—R. Scott Weatherford, Lead Pastor,
First Alliance Church, Calgary

"*Transforming Prayer* is a must-read for not only pastors and church leaders but for everyone who wants to experience the power of prayer. I've known Daniel Henderson for many years and I know that he lives out what he writes. As a pastor we can easily get caught up in the 'doing of the ministry' and leave out the passion of prayer for the ministry. This book will inspire you to go to the next level in your walk with God."

—Matt Fry, Lead Pastor, C3 Church

"The secret of prayer is not what we 'move' God to do for us. Rather, the secret of prayer is how it moves us to become like God. Daniel Henderson has touched a spiritual nerve in the body of Christ, and all of us should respond. We should not be concerned when our prayers are not answered; we should be concerned when we are not transformed into the image of Jesus Christ. May you read this book and be changed accordingly."

—Elmer L. Towns, Co-Founder and Vice President,
Liberty University

"The unique contribution of *Transforming Prayer* by my good friend Daniel Henderson is that it unveils the keys to *prayer that transforms.*"

—Luis Bush, International Facilitator,
Transform World Connections

TRANSFORMING
PRAYER

*How Everything Changes
When You Seek God's Face*

by DANIEL HENDERSON

BETHANY HOUSE PUBLISHERS

Minneapolis, Minnesota

Published by Bethany House Publishers
11400 Hampshire Avenue South
Bloomington, Minnesota 55438

Bethany House Publishers is a division of
Baker Publishing Group, Grand Rapids, Michigan.

Printed in the United States of America

In keeping with biblical principles of creation stewardship, Baker Publishing Group advocates the responsible use of our natural resources. As a member of the Green Press Initiative, our company uses recycled paper when possible. The text paper of this book is comprised of 30% post-consumer waste.

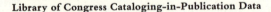

Library of Congress Cataloging-in-Publication Data

Henderson, Daniel.
   Transforming prayer : how everything changes when you seek God's face / Daniel Henderson.
         p.   cm.
   Includes bibliographical references and index.
   Summary: "Examines how Christians can have a more effective and enjoyable prayer life when the emphasis is on worshiping God rather than making requests"—Provided by publisher.
      ISBN 978-0-7642-0851-5 (pbk. : alk. paper) 1. Prayer—Christianity. I. Title.
   BV210.3.H466   2011
   248.3'.2—dc22

2010041166

to D. JUSTIN HENDERSON

. . . my firstborn son, treasured friend,
and colleague in ministry.
Thank you for your help with this project.

to PASTOR PETER LORD

. . . whose teaching first inspired my heart
with a vision to seek God's face.

About the Author

As a pastor for more than twenty-five years, Daniel Henderson brought prayer-based revitalization to several large churches and is now dedicating most of his energy to help congregations across the United States experience renewal and turnaround. He is president of Strategic Renewal, which exists to ignite the heart of the church through personal renewal, congregational revival, and leadership restoration for Christ's glory. In that role he travels extensively, leading churches in renewal experiences, equipping church leaders, and speaking at conferences. He models his renewal focus as Pastor of Prayer and Renewal at Thomas Road Baptist Church and teaches at Liberty University in the areas of prayer, Christian living, and church leadership.

The author of several books, Daniel was on the editorial review team for *Pray!* magazine and serves on the board of the National Association of Evangelicals. He and his wife, Rosemary, have three grown children and live near Lynchburg, Virginia.

For more information, visit *www.strategicrenewal.com*.

Contents

Appendixes

Foreword

At this critical point in church history, there is little time for Christians to be distracted over secondary issues. The challenges of a growing secularization that disparages the gospel of Christ are all too evident to every believer. The Christian church must be stirred to arise and live out the calling Jesus gave us as salt and light.

But how can we see a radical change in the spiritual landscape without a radical return to prayer and the Word by the body of Christ? Human resources and church growth novelties that lead us away from these essentials always prove ineffective at best—and spiritually destructive at worst. Only something sent from heaven itself will overcome the darkness around us so Christ can be seen as the world's only hope.

Every believer knows that the Bible is clear about prayer. God's house will be called a house of prayer. Preaching is essential. Praise, worship, and fellowship are important component parts of the work of the Lord, but His house will be called a house of prayer. Why? Because when believers come to the throne of grace and start seeking God with all their hearts, God has promised—and He can never fail this promise. He has said, "When you call I will answer. Ask and you will receive, seek and you will find, knock and the door will be opened to you." When this happens we are going to see God come and give a renewal of the spirit of prayer, the burden of prayer, and strategies so that all our churches can be houses of prayer.

Then something excellent happens in our lives, our families, and our congregations. Suddenly people are drawn into our churches and needing the Lord. There is a new sense of God in the services, which make them more edifying. And this is always going to happen when people pray.

Every time I set my face to seeking God in a fresh way, God begins to change my heart, my mind, my preaching, and my leadership skills. When any believer commits his or her heart to seeking the Lord, everything is going to change.

It is to be remembered that all revivals in the history of the Christian church that have shaken towns, cities, and countries have all begun with people saying, "We can't take the status quo anymore. We must seek God for something fresh. Let's pray." And then He answers.

Daniel Henderson has been commissioned by God to inspire pastors and churches across the nation to reconsider and commit to Acts 6:4: "But we will devote ourselves to prayer and to the ministry of the word" (ESV). God is wonderfully using Daniel to bring believers together around the country, across denominational lines, to pray for one another and to encourage prayer in our individual churches. This is one of those vital things happening in the body of Christ that is going to bring more of God's blessing in our lives and that will mean the name of Christ will be glorified more than ever before.

As you read *Transforming Prayer,* open your heart to God's voice. You will be both encouraged and inspired to believe again that with God, nothing is impossible.

Jim Cymbala
The Brooklyn Tabernacle Church

A NOTE

For more inspiration related to this book, please go to *www
.transformingprayerbook.com* where you will find video introduc-
tions to each chapter and many additional resources.

For additional information on Daniel Henderson's renewal
ministry, visit *www.strategicrenewal.com*.

HIMSELF

Once it was the blessing,
Now it is the Lord;
Once it was the feeling,
Now it is His Word.
Once His gifts I wanted,
Now the Giver own;
Once I sought for healing,
Now Himself alone.

Once 'twas painful trying,
Now 'tis perfect trust;
Once a half salvation,
Now the uttermost.
Once 'twas ceaseless holding,
Now He holds me fast;
Once 'twas constant drifting,
Now my anchor's cast.

Once 'twas busy planning,
Now 'tis trustful prayer;
Once 'twas anxious caring,
Now He has the care.
Once 'twas what I wanted
Now what Jesus says;
Once 'twas constant asking,
Now 'tis ceaseless praise.

Once it was my working,
His it hence shall be;
Once I tried to use Him,
Now He uses me.
Once the power I wanted,
Now the Mighty One;
Once for self I labored,
Now for Him alone.

Once I hoped in Jesus,
Now I know He's mine;
Once my lamps were dying,
Now they brightly shine.
Once for death I waited,
Now His coming hail;
And my hopes are anchored
Safe within the veil.[1]

—A. B. SIMPSON

Introduction: *The Road to Real Change*

Praying Christians never forget the first time they sought the face of God and experienced the power of a transforming spiritual intimacy. For me, it occurred during my college years. It was a Friday night. I was alone in my dorm room, which was highly unusual as I was typically busy in school activities and dating.

Looking back, I realize the Holy Spirit had been preparing my heart for this moment, as is the case for most believers. The account of Moses speaking to God in deep intimacy "face to face, as a man speaks to his friend" (Exodus 33:11) had recently captivated my heart. One of my professors had been speaking of those times in his life when the presence of God felt so real that if he had opened his eyes it seemed he would be staring God in the face. Honestly, I had never experienced that kind of moment.

I began to thumb through a journal I had maintained over the past year, reading various entries that spoke of my struggles and victories. I reflected on Bible verses that had moved my heart and answers to prayer that were apparent along the way. I was meditating specifically on Philippians 3:7–10 and the message of counting all things as loss in order to know Christ.

That night, as I sat in my simple dorm room, these realities converged as the Holy Spirit stirred my heart with a strange and new spiritual hunger. Without calculation, I found myself flat on my face, pouring out my passionate gratitude and worship to the Savior who knew me, walked with me, guided me, taught me, and loved me with a tender and attentive heart. In those moments, the presence, provision, and power of God in my life became real. Truly, I felt that if I had opened my eyes, I would have been looking at the Holy One . . . face to face.

When I finally got up from the tearstained carpet, over an hour had passed. I had experienced something of His presence and grace that changed me. My heart treasured Christ as never before. A "new normal" had occurred and my soul was re-calibrated to move beyond perfunctory prayer lists and to set my heart to seek His face.

Since this simple encounter I have known the grace of similar intimacy, not only in my personal prayer life but in corporate settings as well. I wish I could say it is a daily experience. One thing I know—once you have tasted this kind of prayer experience, nothing else satisfies and everything else is seen in a new light. But like a caterpillar trying to break out of its cocoon to discover the flight of a butterfly, our goal to make this kind of experience the normal reality of our prayer life does not come easily.

My Confessional

Even though I am writing this book on prayer, I need to confess up front that I am not a natural "prayer guy." I have met plenty of those folks. They come across very spiritual, contemplative, and apparently quite deep. It seems they have emerged from their denominational monastery and should be wearing a robe, swinging an incense censer, and glowing in the dark with the glory of the Almighty. My response to them is a mix of admiration, intimidation, and mystery.

That is not me. You see, prayer is essentially depending on God—and I am a fiercely independent personality. My friends tell me I could be stranded on a deserted island for a week and never realize I am the only one there. Completely absorbed in collecting coconuts, building huts, fishing during the day, playing with fire at night—I would suddenly realize, days later, that no one else was around.

I say often that prayerlessness is our declaration of independence from God. I get that. It is very easy for me to forge ahead on Christian autopilot, relying on the reserves of previous learning and last week's worship, and not abiding in Christ in a constant, moment-by-moment reliance. Beyond this, it is easy to ignore the opportunities for community prayer, thinking I do not need it, or viewing it as a gathering of folks who have nothing else more productive to do with their time.

Longing for More

There must be a lot of people out there sharing my struggle. One of the greater surprises from my almost thirty years of pastoral ministry is how secretly discouraged most Christians are with prayer. We look around church and assume everyone else must be praying more and better than we are. With rare exception, they are not. We hear inspiring sermons from the pulpit on the magnificence of prayer and assume our pastors and church staff members must enjoy extraordinary experiences of prayer together. With rare exception, they do not. We see extensive lists of prayer needs pouring in from broken and desperate people, assuming that someone will engage the power of God in intercessory support for those needs. Too often, they will not.

According to George Barna, the majority of born-again Christians admit that their bi-weekly attendance at worship services is generally the only time they worship God. Eight out of ten believers do not feel they have entered into the presence of God or experienced a connection with Him during the worship service. Half of all believers say they do not feel they have entered the presence of God or experienced a genuine connection with Him in the past year.[1] Whether we are in a church service or going about our weekly routines, it seems that our longings for transformation in Christ's presence remain unsatisfied.

In spite of our common environment of spiritual superficiality, religious routines, and massive distraction, I am convinced that true believers carry an unquenchable appetite for legitimate life change. We hunger for worship encounters with His holy presence that mark us and make us more like Jesus. Deep within we know there is another dimension of Christian living beyond a cultural faith that simply checks in with God at church or in times of crisis. We are tired of feeling bored, inept, confused, frustrated, or weary, in any sense, with the idea of prayer. We envision the power of the living Christ and His gospel inflaming our hearts to serve as agents of real transformation in this society. We yearn for real change but know that somehow it must begin within us.

Deep within we know there is another dimension of Christian living beyond a cultural faith that simply checks in with God at church or in times of crisis.

Testimony, Teaching, and Trophy Case

I admit much has been written on prayer—perhaps too much. On one hand, I feel a bit convicted by adding more information to the pile of prayer material that is already available, whether through great devotional classics, contemporary authors, or online resources. However, I am passionate about helping you discover what I have seen thousands experience as they have learned the power of an approach to prayer that is truly transformational.

As a result, this book is part testimony, part teaching, and part trophy case. You will experience the power of testimony because this subject, other than the truth of the gospel, has transformed my life more than any other in my four decades of following Christ. You will enjoy helpful teaching as biblical truth unfolds in order to transform your own prayer life. You will find yourself exploring a trophy case of changed lives as I share the stories of those who have also experienced a fresh approach to prayer.

As I write, I can imagine a Spirit-instigated tidal wave of engaging and enduring prayer that changes our lives as "times of refreshing" come from the presence of the Lord. I hope you will imagine with me as we journey together into a renewed understanding of the power of Christ who can still transform our lives and our world through the reality of prayer.

PART ONE

THE VISION *for a* TRANSFORMED LIFE

CHAPTER 1

Beyond a "Grocery List" of Needs

Prayer [is] intimacy with God
that leads to the fulfillment of his purposes.

ALVIN REID

And when you pray, do not use vain repetitions as the heathen do.
For they think that they will be heard for their many words.

JESUS—MATTHEW 6:7

My dad taught me how to play golf. He was the classic old duffer. I am not sure he ever took lessons—but growing up, golf gave us quality time together, so we played quite often, just not well. Today, I am advancing my father's legacy of mediocre golf. It is what I learned from his example.

My son Jordan is a worship pastor, and very good at what he does. His skills in worship did not occur because he was standing under a tree one day and a "worship apple" fell on his head, causing him to suddenly start singing Chris Tomlin songs. He learned to worship through observing others. He was exposed to some great worship pastors and profound worship experiences in his early years. He went on to earn his degree in worship ministries. Much of what he does today is a result of those personal and corporate models that he experienced growing up.

We all learn many of the essential skills of life through the model of others we love and respect. Some skills allow us to excel and become contributors to others. However, we can also learn ineptitude through the repetition of mindless tradition or dysfunction.

This leads to a core inquiry. Who taught you to pray? Has anyone provided a positive and life-changing model of prayer for you? Do you feel that you even know how to pray effectively? What is the purpose behind your praying? Is it working for you? Are you sure it is a biblical approach? On the other hand, are you simply doing what you have seen others do, wondering if there might be more to the reality of prayer than you have experienced so far in your life?

Unlearning Prayer

Theologian D. A. Carson makes the observation: "Christians learn to pray by listening to those around them."[1] I must admit that I had to unlearn prayer. While I was grateful for some of the faithful Christians I knew during my early years, I am not sure their model of prayer really hit the mark or made much of a difference in helping me learn a biblical, life-transforming way to pray.

The earliest memories of my struggle with prayer go back to my elementary school days. I had a serious "drug problem." My parents drug me to the old-fashioned Wednesday night prayer meeting almost every week—especially when I had misbehaved. Perhaps they viewed it as a tool to reform me. To me, it was punishment.

Every Wednesday evening at seven, very sincere and devoted (mostly senior) saints would gather. The song leader would try to stir the group with some familiar hymns—four or five meaty verses each. Eventually, another man would share a devotion of sorts. Seldom did it relate to prayer, and I suspected he threw it together on the way to the prayer meeting in his pickup truck.

Then the leader would ask the dreaded question: "Does anyone have any prayer requests?" On cue, almost everyone pulled out their yellow pads and blue Bic pens to capture the finer details of each request. They were fully devoted to this ritual with good hearts and a genuine willingness to intercede for one another.

Unfortunately, for me, it seemed like everyone in the country must have had an ingrown toenail, a slipped disc, a cousin with cancer, or a friend in financial crisis. The requests went on and on. I got more depressed and sleepy as this part of the meeting dragged out, often for forty-five minutes or more.

Occasionally, some juicy gossip made its way into the conversation. Someone would suggest an "unspoken prayer request" for Deacon Charlie. Upon further review, we discovered that Charlie had separated from his wife, Matilda. Soon the discussion uncovered the shocking news that Matilda was having an affair with the piano player's husband. The piano player was on the verge of suicide (another prayer request). No surprise, Charlie and Matilda were struggling—because we then learned that their oldest son was a drug addict, their daughter was pregnant out of wedlock, and a third cousin on Charlie's side was a convicted car thief. Someone even suggested that their dog had rabies.

It seemed like everyone in the country must have had an ingrown toenail, a slipped disc, a cousin with cancer, or a friend in financial crisis. The requests went on and on.

The exhaustive requests continued until someone happened to glance at their watch and exclaim, "Oh, we're almost out of time! We'd better pray." Hurriedly, we would slide our folding chairs into smaller circles, yellow pads in hand, and start praying for the myriad of documented needs.

Beyond "Bless" and "Be With"

I hate to say it, but it seemed to me that if you took the words *bless* and *be with* out of their prayer vocabulary, no one would have had anything to say. The prayers commenced in systematic fashion as we went down the list: "Bless this, bless that—be with him, be with her. . . ." And they seemed to pick up the pace as the final minutes of the allotted time ticked away.

As we finished this flurry of *bless*es and *be with*s, the group

would break out in a rousing round of "Sweet Hour of Prayer."
Today I love this classic hymn, but back then it sounded like
a sanctified version of "Ninety-Nine Bottles of Beer on the
Wall"—and seemed to drag on just as long.

The leader would then announce, "Thanks for coming.
We'll see you next week!" In my immature, confused, and quite
bored mind, I thought, *No thanks, I hope to stay home and watch*
Hogan's Heroes.

Sincere but Stuck

In spite of my skewed view of these old-fashioned prayer
times, I know these dear saints were sincere and committed.
At least they were at a prayer meeting. Most of the flock was
at the softball league, the PTA meetings, out to eat at the local
Mexican restaurant, or home watching *Hogan's Heroes.*

This praying minority would seldom miss a week. As much
as I did not appreciate their pattern of prayer, I loved their hearts
and willingness to persevere. These prayer warriors really did
make prayer a priority. They saw some wonderful answers to
prayer and were careful to thank the Lord for it all. It did seem,
however, that they were inadvertently stuck in a long, deep
prayer rut.

Of course, our prayer requests are a vital part of prayer. The
Bible is clear about the need to ask God for things and share
our burdens with one another. The rut occurs when we allow
requests to serve as the foundation of our praying: focusing
on our problems rather than actually engaging with God in a
multifaceted biblical prayer experience.

Clearly, the request-based approach just did not work for me.
I have learned that it has not worked for many seeking Christians. This dissatisfaction led me to a growing and life-changing
understanding of what I call worship-based prayer. It was not
a new discovery but a simple revelation of what is clear in the
Scriptures as a positive alternative to "grocery-list" praying. This
approach has transformed my life and the lives of thousands I
have encountered who have made this vital discovery.

What Is Worship-Based Prayer?

Worship is the response of all we are to the revelation of all God is. J. Oswald Sanders describes worship as "the loving ascription of praise to God for what He is, both in Himself and in His ways. It is the bowing of the innermost spirit in deep humility and reverence before Him."[2]

Worship-based prayer seeks the face of God before the hand of God. God's face is the essence of who He is. God's hand is the blessing of what He does. God's face represents His person and presence. God's hand expresses His provision for needs in our lives. I have learned that if all we ever do is seek God's hand, we may miss His face; but if we seek His face, He will be glad to open His hand and satisfy the deepest desires of our hearts.

If all we ever do is seek God's hand, we may miss His face; but if we seek His face, He will be glad to open His hand and satisfy the deepest desires of our hearts.

This approach to prayer always begins with a focus on biblical, Spirit-empowered worship. It is distinctively different from the traditional approach that emphasizes prayer requests and long lists of needs as the foundation of prayer. Christ taught a worship-based approach to prayer. It is modeled by many biblical personalities. It is fueled by scriptural truth in every case. Worship-based prayer ignites a desire for spiritual intimacy and personal transformation. In the discovery of these realities, a Christian is then empowered and enlightened to pray about issues and needs in a whole new way.

What Worship-Based Prayer Is Not

As you prepare for this journey of discovery about the principles and practices of worship-based prayer, let me tell you what worship-based prayer is NOT.

- **It is not a new method of prayer.** While the discovery has been fresh for many in this generation, it is an approach to prayer that is as old as the Scriptures.

- **It is not worship-ONLY prayer.** Biblical, balanced prayer has many expressions. This is not about restricting your prayer life only to worship, but about rekindling your prayer life from a foundation of worship to more fully enjoy and experience confession, requests, intercession, and warfare prayers.

- **It does not eliminate requests.** Our Father commands and compels us to call on Him—and He promises to answer. Requests are a vital part of prayer. However, requests without the proper foundation and framework can miss the mark. Worship-based prayer helps us understand the context, conditions, and ultimate conclusion of all our prayer requests.

- **It is not complicated.** While the term may sound a bit different, the approach is not difficult. Ultimately, it is as pure as opening the Scriptures and your soul in Spirit-led communion with Christ and allowing Him to set the agenda for every prayer time you enjoy. By the time you finish this book, I hope to inspire and equip you to experience the power of seeking God's face in ways that will truly transform your prayers and your life.

Stories of Transformation

As a pastor, I have seen firsthand the power of worship-based prayer to bring healing and restoration to hurting congregations. I have watched it reinvent a staid, traditional church into a church-planting, mission-oriented force. Most thrilling is the fact that thousands of believers have experienced a revived love for Christ and a renewed passion for Spirit-empowered ministry.

In October 1995, Lori gave her life to Jesus Christ. A few months later, she signed up to attend a prayer event sponsored by the women of our church. They were going away to pray for three days, with no agenda. This was a big stretch for a baby Christian.

At the time, her song repertoire consisted of the chorus of "Amazing Grace" and "Jesus Loves Me." She writes, "I wouldn't have been able to find a book of the Bible other than Genesis if you'd paid me. And as you might imagine, I would never dream of lifting up my hands as I had seen once in one of those 'weird churches.' "

However, God used that weekend to transform her life. She learned how to open the Bible and worship God as the majestic, sovereign, and mighty One who is worthy of praise. She saw Him take hurting people and give them peace, hope, and joy. After experiencing the deep, deep love of Christ that weekend, her life has never been the same.

In the ensuing years, Lori became the ministry director of Strategic Renewal, the nonprofit organization I founded, teaching the principles of worship-based prayer to hundreds of churches around the nation. Today she leads the prayer ministry at a growing congregation in Northern California. God is using her in profound ways. Blessings continue to pour into her life, family, and ministry all because one day, as a new believer, she stepped into a praying church and encountered a life-transforming moment in His presence.[3]

Randy, a doctor from California, was intrigued by the idea of learning to pray a new way. Like Lori, he also decided to attend a prayer retreat that would feature extended time with opened Bibles, spontaneous singing, and free-flowing worship. Prior to the retreat, he was asking, "What am I going to talk to God about for three days?" Afterward he noted, "I was asking the wrong question. What I should have said was, 'What was God going to talk to me about for three days?' " Although an established Christian, he learned that prayer is a two-way conversation, and God wanted to start the conversation from His Word, initiating a deep and rich experience of worship as the foundation of prayer. Randy's prayer life has never been the same.

Dixie was a long-time staff member at her Baptist church. Through teaching, modeling, and her willingness to learn, she moved from a request-based to a worship-based approach to prayer. She elaborates on the first time she made the discovery: "What I experienced was fresh and new to me. I became very aware of the Lord's presence in the midst of the worship. He filled me so full of himself and loved on me. He caused me to hunger for more of Him. I knew I wanted to be clean in His presence because He shone light on the places I needed to confess. I gladly gave myself up, and He just continued to pour into me joy, peace, contentment, and eagerness to worship Him more."

Dixie testifies, "I have not been the same since. My personal and corporate times of worship are much richer and sweeter. I now know the real meaning of a romance with Jesus. I don't just love Him; I am *in* love with Him. How amazing to know that my worship and praying are pleasing to Him. As I praise Him for who He is, all the concerns and questions of my life are laid to rest."

Let the Adventure Begin

Peter Lord, one of my personal mentors and a pastor for over five decades, states, "Most Christians pray out of crisis or from a grocery list—period." His point is that God has much more for us in our walk with Him when we learn to seek His face, not just His hand. This is the discovery so many are making today in their relationship with Christ.

"Most Christians pray out of crisis or from a grocery list—period."

Like Lori, Randy, and Dixie, perhaps you are eager to move beyond a grocery-list approach to prayer. Maybe you have felt the stirring of a deep dissatisfaction over your attempts to learn to pray. As you read these pages with an open heart, perhaps your soul resonates with the hope of new possibilities in your walk with God.

Join me as we hear the call of God to our hearts—"Seek My face" (Psalm 27:8)—and readily respond, "Your face, Lord, I will seek." When this becomes the passion and pattern of our lives, transformation occurs.

CHAPTER 2

The Potential for Transformation

Everyone thinks of changing the world,
but no one thinks of changing himself.
LEO TOLSTOY

Now when they saw the boldness of Peter and John,
and perceived that they were uneducated and untrained men,
they marveled.
And they realized that they had been with Jesus.
ACTS 4:13

Years ago, I remember hearing the story of a father who was relaxing as he read the newspaper in the den after dinner. All the while, his young son persisted in interrupting him, wanting the father to play. After numerous attempts to occupy the boy with something else, the father experienced what he considered a stroke of genius. Discovering a page from the newspaper with a full-size map of the world, he tore it into small pieces. Handing them to his son, he made the challenge, "When you put this map of the world back together, we will go out and play."

Assuming he had occupied his son for a long while, he resumed his reading. However, a few minutes later, the boy returned with the map taped together. Shocked that his son knew this much about geography, he asked how the boy had recreated the map so quickly.

The little boy replied, "It was easy. There is a picture of a man on the back. When I got the man right, I got the world right."

Too many times we become preoccupied with the tools, techniques, and even the finer points of theology when it comes to prayer. All of these are helpful, but prayer is not so much an issue of fine-tuning the regimens but of enjoying the relationship. It is not so much about fixing all the peripheral issues of our lives through prayer, but allowing God to change us through prayer. When we get the man right, by His transforming grace, it is amazing how so many other things seem to line up and make sense.

Imagine What God Could Do!

For several years, the church I pastored in Northern California hosted a conference called "Imagine What God Could Do!" Hundreds of pastors and parishioners came every year from dozens of states to learn more about the transforming power of prayer in individual lives, homes, and churches. The worship at these conferences was powerful. The teaching from our guest speakers and local workshop leaders proved to be very helpful. The prayer times, which were a core element of the conference, proved to be a distinctive feature and real highlight.

Yet the most frequent feedback we received from conference attendees had nothing to do with the details or activities of the conference. The most positive comments always related to the lives of the church members hosting the conference. In the course of interacting with the people of our church, others saw the changes, heard the stories, and left hungry for the same kind of transformation. I was the "paid salesman" for worship-based prayer. They were the "satisfied customers." The living out of the message made more of a lasting impact than words from the pulpit. It is hard to ignore the reality of a transformed life.

This change was manifested in contagious spiritual passion for Christ, healed marriages, restored families, deliverance from habitual sin, divine calling to greater ministry, deeper compassion for non-believers, and a fresh zeal for world missions. What created this spiritual movement? Not a program. Not a pastor. Not some new church-growth strategy. All of these blessings came because people learned to seek the face of God in prayer.

During my eleven years as the pastor, we enjoyed thirty-three three-day prayer summits, going away to a camp or retreat center with no agenda but to pray. These gatherings involved a guided approach to spontaneous Scripture reading, singing, and responsive prayer in a variety of large-group, small-group, and individual settings. These summits spawned dozens of weekly small-group prayer gatherings, a World Prayer Center, and a weekly church-wide prayer experience called Fresh Encounter that attracted hundreds. Personal prayer lives were ignited and changed as well. Ultimately things changed because people changed.

Ultimately things changed because people changed.

The Fruit of Transforming Prayer

In recent years, I have enjoyed the privilege of friendship and shared ministry with Jim Cymbala, pastor of The Brooklyn Tabernacle in Brooklyn, New York. We are working together to encourage pastors and help them embrace a greater sense of their calling to prayer and the ministry of the Word (Acts 6:4).[1]

I have heard Pastor Cymbala say many times that we will not one day stand before Christ to announce the *size* of our ministry, but to give an account of the *substance* of our ministry. Christ's evaluation, both now and in eternity, is based upon the fruit evidenced in the lives of the people to whom we minister.

As I have watched the power of worship-based prayer transform hundreds of lives, I have seen some very specific fruit. I long for more of this fruit in my life and the lives of everyone I influence. I grieve when I fall short of this fruit. I pray for a greater vision and passion for fruit in my life and the lives of others.

What does this fruit look like? Here is a summary of what I have seen occur as people learn to seek God's face:

God is glorified!—One of the great results of transforming prayer is that people recognize God at work because they have joined Him in that work through their prayers. Their hearts are sensitized to His presence, His power, and His purposes. Their lips are free to recognize Him as the source of all good things. Their hearts are eager to cry out, "Not unto us, O Lord, not unto us, but to Your name give glory!" (Psalm 115:1).

For people who fail to pray, everything is a coincidence that has little recognition of God at work. For those who pray, everything is a co-incident, as they have joined the Lord in His work through the privilege of prayer. The principle is simple. When we pray, God gets the thanks and the credit for what happens.

We are sanctified!—*Sanctified.* Did you notice that word in the morning paper today? Of course not. It is not a word in common use, but it packs a powerful meaning. It means to be "set apart" to God. It means God is working in me, around me, and through me to make me holy, more like Jesus.

> *Praying Christians, while not perfect, are growing every day to the point that they act, think, speak, and serve like Jesus.*

The great fruit of transforming prayer is that praying Christians, while not perfect, are growing every day to the point that they act, think, speak, and serve like Jesus.

The church is edified!—When I first came to the church in Northern California, I followed a godly predecessor who served for forty years as their senior pastor. This left a great heritage, for which I was very grateful. It also left a very traditional and older church. These wonderful saints cherished the days of the past and felt trepidation as they faced the inevitability of change in the future.

Five years later, at one of our conferences, a visiting pastor from New York commented, "These are the youngest old people I have ever seen." This was evidence that when transformation occurs within hearts, ignited by the truth and presence of Christ, everything else begins to change for the sake of the health of the church and the fulfillment of the mission.

Jude 20 says, "But you, beloved, building yourselves up on your most holy faith, praying in the Holy Spirit. . . ." The Amplified version elaborates, "But you, beloved, build yourselves up [founded] on your most holy faith [make progress, rise like an edifice higher and higher], praying in the Holy Spirit." To say that the church is "edified" means that the lives, marriages, families, and ministries of the church are built up, made strong and healthy—through biblical prayer, in the power of the Holy Spirit.

The world is mystified!—Over the years, we have heard significant debate about the best way to reach the unchurched and what influences the hearts of unbelievers who attend our church services. First Corinthians 14:25 is the only verse in the New Testament that speaks specifically to the experience of an unbeliever coming into a church service. In essence, when the Spirit is working among God's people and the truth is honored in their midst, it says that the unbeliever sees this in the lives of believers and "the secrets of his heart are revealed; and so, falling down on his face, he will worship God and report that God is truly among you." I believe this is a clear description of the glory (manifest presence) of Christ among His people.

The early disciples, who "filled Jerusalem" with their doctrine and "turned the world upside down" (Acts 5:28; 17:6), truly mystified the religious people of the day. When the Jewish leaders interrogated Peter and John, it was said, "Now when they saw the boldness of Peter and John, and perceived that they were uneducated and untrained men, they marveled. And they realized that they had been with Jesus" (Acts 4:13).

The world is not transformed by relevant Christians, strategic Christians, visionary Christians, leadership-savvy Christians, wealthy Christians, attractive Christians, educated Christians, active Christians, or articulate Christians. These are all interesting qualities, and might be helpful on occasion—especially in building big religious organizations and selling books.

Ultimately, the world is transformed by sanctified Christians through whom the life of Jesus becomes a mystifying manifestation. As Paul said, "For it is the God who commanded light to shine out of darkness, who has shone in our hearts to give the light of the knowledge of the glory of God in the face of Jesus Christ. But we have this treasure in earthen vessels, that the excellence of the power may be of God and not of us" (2 Corinthians 4:6–7). People changed by Jesus cannot help but change the world.

The enemy is notified!—This is not a book on spiritual warfare, but at this point I want to remind you that Satan is not omniscient. He is supernatural and powerful, and supported by myriads of demonic forces, but he cannot read our thoughts. The best he can do is observe our behavior, eavesdrop on our conversations, and implement a strategy to send his fiery darts against our minds—based on his understanding of our vulnerabilities and habits.

When we are in the habit of experiencing transformation as we seek God's face, the enemy's efforts to defeat, discourage, distract, or destroy us are met with the reality of our Christ-ward focus and the victory that comes from intimacy with Jesus. To Satan's dismay, he sees us praying, trusting God, and becoming more like our Lord as we do so. He is notified that we are engaged in a pursuit of the promises of transformation and impact for the Savior.

Make Us Right!

So many times, we are like the little boy with cut-up newspaper pieces strewn around him. The nature of life, the manipulations of other people, and the spiritual attacks on our souls leave us feeling like we are holding a jumbled pile of nonsense that has no rhyme or reason to it. But when our Savior "puts the man together" to make us right first, then in so many ways the world comes together.

God is glorified. We are sanctified. The church is edified. The world is mystified. The enemy is notified.

I Stopped Praying for Four Years:
A Trophy of Transformation

by BILL L.—MISSIONARY, SPAIN

Part of me died on December 10, 2001, when my lifelong friend passed away. In my grief, I viewed God as good but distant. I had no intimacy with Him and did not feel His love; therefore, I had little love for anyone else. I concluded that God was going to do whatever He wanted to do with no regard for my prayers. Since there was absolutely zero reason to pray, I stopped praying for four years.

At the core of my prayerlessness was a mix of pride and lies. Pride caused me to refuse to ask God for His help until I had exhausted all of my own capacities. I studied, ministered, and pursued life-change by the sweat of my brow. The lies I believed about God were based on my personal experience rather than believing the truth about God as revealed in Scripture. I saw Him as vindictive, not as a loving Father. But God used worship-based prayer as a catalyst to bring me back to himself.

Worship-based prayer did more than teach me to pray; it revealed who God is. As I spent time seeing God and learning what it meant to seek His face, I experienced His powerful presence and was transformed. While in the presence of God, the Holy Spirit reveals to a heart in five seconds that which can never be accomplished through years of human effort. Strangely, I began to *enjoy* prayer. As God changed my view of prayer, He also changed my view of himself. The more I learned about God's true character, the more I wanted to pray. I longed to trust in God, have greater faith, and to know Him better. Prayer became a cycle of growth in the pursuit of God.

Now when I pray, I intercede on the basis of God's character; and when I doubt, I cling to one of His attributes. By the time I get around to talking to God about my situation, He has already given me a peace that transcends all understanding. Prayer malfunctions when the worship aspects are removed, but worship-based prayer is effective because it takes our eyes off of ourselves or our situations and focuses them where they should be—on the Most High God.

CHAPTER 3

What Is Blocking the Breakthrough?

All true prayer
Exists for the glory of God
And is
Based in the worship of God
Focused on the face of God
Shaped by the Word of God
Inspired by the Spirit of God
Offered through the Son of God
Aimed for the Will of God
Experienced by true children of God

DANIEL HENDERSON

Whom have I in heaven but You?
And there is none upon earth that I desire besides You.
My flesh and my heart fail;
But God is the strength of my heart and my portion forever.

PSALM 73:25–26

Connie knew many of the great truths about prayer from childhood. Growing up in a pastor's home, she attended virtually every church service and countless prayer meetings. She saw evidence of the blessings of prayer in the lives of some of the people in the church, but personally never really felt anything transformational from her experiences with prayer.

"Prayer was simply asking, pleading, seeking action from God on one's own behalf or on the behalf of others," Connie says. "I participated dutifully but did not recognize the hole in my heart as the lack of a truly personal, intimate relationship with God. He was there, but distant, and I did not know life could be any different. I did not know God's purpose for prayer."

She elaborates, "I had become a robot-like Christian—doing what was expected, regularly attending church, taking notes on the sermon, serving where asked, saying the right things, quoting someone else's experiences, attending fill-in-the-blank Bible studies, and witnessing from someone else's prepared material. In short, I looked okay—but inside I felt a vast empty, consuming unrest. No matter what I did, nothing was enough or took away the fear of being unloved or rejected."

Later in this chapter, Connie will describe how her life was transformed. But why is her experience common for so many who attend church and seek to develop an authentic walk with God? What barriers exist that keep us from the transformational power of prayer the Lord intended for us?

Let's be honest. Most of us struggle to feel satisfied in our prayer lives. The great promises of prayer are true, but many don't experience them. Even pastors are trying to find their way when it comes to prayer. One study found that only 16 percent of Protestant ministers across the country are very satisfied with their personal prayer life. Another 47 percent are somewhat satisfied; 30 percent are somewhat dissatisfied; and 7 percent are very dissatisfied with their prayer lives.[1]

Barriers to Blessing

If prayer is such a vital tool for transformation, why is it so difficult for so many people? Why does this divinely intended blessing remain a burden for many believers? As J. Oswald Sanders noted, "We sometimes pay lip service to the delight and power of prayer. We call it indispensable, we know the Scriptures call for it. Yet we often fail to pray."[2]

Spiritual Warfare

Clearly, prayer is an area where believers experience spiritual warfare. Our spiritual enemy is fully aware of the power and promises available to us in prayer. He knows that every major spiritual revival began with prayer. He knows we are all called to be "praying menaces" to his cause. Therefore, he fights us from every angle to keep us from praying effectively. The devil launches his weapons of mass distraction to keep us too preoccupied with other things to take time to really connect with God. He bombards us with his fiery darts of doubt to keep us from praying in faith to the One who is "a rewarder of those who diligently seek Him" (Hebrews 11:6). Our enemy seeks to discourage us at every turn because he is threatened by believers and congregations that take prayer seriously and pursue Christ passionately.

Fear of Intimacy

Some falter in prayer because of a fear of intimacy. I often say that we live in a culture of spiritual AIDS (Acute Intimacy Deficiency Syndrome). Some of us still carry the baggage from parents or other authority figures in our childhood who were distant, negligent, or even abusive. These experiences can leave us with distaste for emotional vulnerability and transparency. We protect ourselves from getting too close to anyone, even God.

We live in a culture of spiritual AIDS (Acute Intimacy Deficiency Syndrome).

Others simply embrace erroneous views of God's character that keep them at a distance from their self-styled deity who is mysteriously remote, unpredictably angry, and impossible to please. We read the biblical texts that tell us that "it is good for me to draw near to God" (Psalm 73:28) and that we should "draw near with a true heart in full assurance of faith" (Hebrews 10:22). We read the promise that if we draw near to God He will draw near to us (James 4:8). Yet the reality of this seems threatening and unachievable.

Misguided Focus

Many of us maintain a misguided focus in our prayers and miss the life-giving reality God intended. Instead of our first resolve, we view prayer as our last resort. We see prayer as our spiritual e-mail sent to God, with instructions as to how He should manage the affairs of our life each day. We attempt to use prayer to get our will done in heaven rather than His will done on earth. When one tries to use a hammer to baste a turkey or a light bulb to brush our hair, the result is frustration and failure. It is imperative that we have a clear understanding of the foundation and focus of prayer as found in the "owners' manual": Scripture.

> *Instead of our first resolve, we view prayer as our last resort.*

When this focus becomes clear and correct, God works powerfully for new believers, established Christians, and even respected spiritual leaders. R. A. Torrey, who was God's instrument to bring revival to many parts of the world in the early 1900s, testified that an utter transformation came into his experience when he learned not only to pray and return thanks, but to worship—asking nothing of God, seeking nothing from Him, occupied with himself, and satisfied with himself.[3] At any point in our lives, the Lord can refocus our prayers with powerful results.

Counterproductive Tradition

Countless believers have learned to pray, from a counterproductive tradition, forms of prayer passed down through the generations without much critical evaluation and biblical investigation. Some traditions in prayer rely mainly on "prayer lists" and others on rote expressions, rather than upon the leading of the Holy Spirit. The primary content of many prayer gatherings is juicy information about other people rather than the foundation of God's Word. We tend more toward discussions about the problems of people than the real experiences of the presence of the Problem Solver. Most believers know that something is amiss in these gatherings, even if they cannot put their finger on it. As a result, individuals and congregations flounder in their commitment and enjoyment of prayer. My friend David Butts, chairperson of America's National Prayer Committee, says, "The reason most people do not attend prayer meetings at their church is that they have been to prayer meetings at their church."

Boredom

All of these factors can fuel a deep-seated feeling of boredom. As a Christ-follower for over forty years, I am resolute to banish boredom from my prayer life. As a pastor for almost thirty years, having led multiple weekly prayer times, I have declared war on sleepy prayer meetings. I wrote an entire book on the need for creativity in prayer and the reality that God is not the author of boredom, especially when we are conversing with Him.[4] Yet many of us have all but given up our high expectations about prayer. For many, prayer has become a real yawner—and that has to change before transformation can occur.

Lack of Positive Models

One colossal reason we have not experienced transforming prayer is the lack of positive models. I have learned that people do not arrive at a new, powerful, and life-changing place in their prayer life through information. It happens more by "infection." It is not accomplished through explanation, but by experience.

D. A. Carson confirms this truth when he writes, "Many facets of Christian discipleship, not the least prayer, are more effectively passed on by modeling than by formal teaching. Good praying is more easily caught than taught. . . . We should choose models from whom we can learn."[5] Choosing models is one thing. Finding a biblical one is another. It seems the venues and opportunities for the kind of praying that leaves us forever changed are few and far between. Yet if we have a hunger to learn, ask God to open the doors, and seek a mentoring opportunity in prayer, I believe God will show us how we can connect with a context for deeper motivation and growth. In my own journey, I've had to be very proactive and even creative to find models and mentors.

Contexts for Breakthrough

For the past decade, I have taken hundreds of fellow leaders, church members, and students to the Tuesday night prayer meetings at The Brooklyn Tabernacle. It is not the only model, but probably the most compelling example of a church in the United States where believers really know how to pray. (Alternatively, there are countless models in other countries like South Korea and in areas of the world where Christians face persecution, like China.) Under the leadership of Pastor Jim Cymbala, four thousand gather every Tuesday night, simply to seek the Lord and enjoy the abundance of His presence. Prayer is the engine that drives all the ministries of this high-impact church.

> *"The heart cannot taste what the eyes have not seen."*

I heard a Brazilian proverb years ago: "The heart cannot taste what the eyes have not seen." This experience of praying with a pastor, church, and congregation that authentically value the priority and power of prayer has accomplished much to help me and many other believers understand a truly biblical paradigm.

Today, my passion is to serve as a "spiritual pyromaniac," traveling to churches and conferences, demonstrating the power of seeking God's face, and leading prayer experiences that establish a fresh, life-transforming approach to prayer. This is my small way of serving others with some modeling and mentoring experiences. It is exhilarating beyond words, week after week, to see the lights come on for people who discover that the promises and power of prayer can be real—and that prayer can change things, starting with our own hearts.

Changed Forever

In spite of the frustrations and fears she shared earlier in this chapter, Connie took a radical step in the early nineties and attended a three-day event hosted by her local church at a nearby Christian campground. There would be no agenda, no lists, no speakers, and no special music. This experience of Scripture-fed,

Spirit-led, worship-based prayer was scary at first but has been the secret to personal transformation for her ever since.

In her own words, she testifies of this first encounter: "I learned that true prayer and worship involves the whole being—spirit, soul, and body. My spirit was soaring and experiencing God's presence. My soul was receiving the love of God in new ways; peace and well-being were welling up in me as a flood. My eyes were weeping, my hands were lifted. I sang with abandon as I knelt before God—in public. My heart felt it would burst with the love of God, both received and given. This was worship-based prayer. All this was new to me, and it was wonderful!"

In describing her Christian life today, she says, "My 'walk' was changed forever. Actually, my whole being and attitude was changed. I did not want to go back to a casual relationship with God. I had discovered that prayer truly has only two purposes. First, it is the means to developing a true love relationship with God by communication with Him, not to get His 'stuff' but to get to know Him more deeply. Prayer is intended to develop a *two-way* love relationship. Second, it is to receive His assignments for me, both daily and long term—by listening to Him—then acting, not only in how I live but also in how I pray for myself and others."

She concludes, "God loves me and will take care of all my needs but only *I* can develop my love for Him. That will be done only as I am determined to know who He is, His character, His desires, and to concentrate on Him, not on what I want or think I need. As I commune with Him based and grounded in worship, He reveals himself to me in new and wonderful ways."

God has used Connie to organize a variety of prayer events and gatherings since those early days of personal transformation. Her prayer conferences have attracted hundreds. It all began when she learned to seek His face, not just His hand.

Perhaps like Connie, you are longing for lasting alterations in your spiritual journey and life direction as you learn to seek the face of God. The promises are real. The potential is unfathomable. The principles are proven. Christ is extending the invitation to your heart. Right here. Right now.

A Changed Life and Vocation:
A Trophy of Transformation

Jeff was raised in the church—and confesses that he was at the building every time the doors were opened, including the midweek prayer times. By his early thirties, Jeff became a rising star as a financial planner. Like many believers, Jeff loved Bible study and conservative values but felt a void in his intimacy with Christ.

In 2002, Jeff and his wife, Holly, visited a weekly worship-based prayer service at a church in their area. In describing this encounter, he writes, "We were blown away that prayer times could be that exciting and remarkable. It was life-giving and we could not wait to come back the following week. It changed my perspective about God and how to pray to Him." He began to sense an awakening in his heart, not just to know about the Lord at an intellectual level, but to know the Lord in a transforming intimacy.

But more changes were to come. Jeff testifies, "It turned my family inside out as we began to pray in a new way. In fact, worship-based prayer quickly turned the direction of my life, with a desire to change vocations. I had experienced earthly success, but I wanted to experience significance. Eventually, that led to moving across the country and serving as an executive pastor. In all of these decisions, the driving force is that I want to have others encounter Jesus in a different way and one that will allow people to see Him for who He really is—His face and not just His hand. I have seen pastors, missionaries, marriages, and many individual lives turned around by the reality of seeking Christ in prayer."

CHAPTER 4

Face Time!

God thirsts to be thirsted after.

ST. AUGUSTINE

The Lord bless you and keep you;
The Lord make His face shine upon you,
And be gracious to you;
The Lord lift up His countenance upon you,
And give you peace.

NUMBERS 6:24–26

I love "face time"—with certain people. When I get face time with my wife, children, family members, and good friends, it is always meaningful and enriching.

Of course, I also dread face time with certain people. This category would include self-important and insecure people who always talk about themselves. I avoid face time with chronically negative people. I prefer not to have face time with police officers who have pulled me over for speeding. I don't look forward to face time with the doctor someday when he has to give me some bad news about my body or the health of a loved one.

Face time can be good or bad, depending on whom we are facing and the nature of the encounter. People far from God avoid face time with the Almighty—at least on this earth. Someday, everyone—the righteous and the unrighteous—will have some personal face time with the risen and reigning Christ.

> *The idea of God's face is one of the most powerful, life-changing themes in the Bible.*

The idea of God's face is one of the most powerful, life-changing themes in the Bible. Still, many live their entire lives with minimal emphasis on face time with God. Perhaps they don't understand the incredible opportunity because they've never experienced it. Maybe they don't feel the need. Maybe prayer time is just too rushed. But face time with God is the refreshment the human soul so desperately needs. And like temperature, pulse, and blood pressure tests we encounter when we visit the doctor, face time tells us how we are really doing. If we get nothing else from this book, we must get this.

What's in a Face?

What is meant by *face*? It is the representation of the real essence and character of a person. It is the unique identifying characteristic of an individual. It is also the key to really getting to know someone. Proverbs 15:13 says, "A happy heart makes the face cheerful" (NIV). Just as the eyes are the windows to the soul, so a face is the canvas of the heart and personality. Oscar Wilde said, "A man's face is his autobiography."

In the Scriptures, we are encouraged to seek God's face. Certainly the Bible says that God is Spirit (John 4:24). He is "eternal, immortal, invisible" (1 Timothy 1:17). He dwells in "unapproachable light" (1 Timothy 6:16). Yet the Bible calls us to an intimate encounter and speaks of those who have communed with Almighty God face-to-face.

God's face refers to His holy, intimate presence manifested to humans on earth. In the ultimate sense, we cannot experience His full, unrestrained presence and live to tell about it. Yet He reveals himself to us to the degree that we have the capacity—because He wants us to know and experience Him, and He created us for this very purpose.

If you have ever been away from someone you love for an extended period, you know the exhilaration of seeing that person again. While you may notice his clothes or hair or cologne—your real joy is to look again into his eyes and gaze upon his face. This image of a joyful eye-to-eye reunion reminds us again of the spiritual longings of our heart toward God.

As early as Adam and Eve in the garden of Eden, it says that because of their sin they "hid themselves from the presence [literally, *face*] of the Lord God" (Genesis 3:8). They had previously communed with His holy presence, and their consciences alerted them immediately that their behavior had violated the intimacy God created them to enjoy.

Jacob encountered the presence of God as he wrestled with the Lord all night long. By morning his name (core identity) was changed to *Israel* and he limped from that moment on. He said of that experience, "I have seen God face to face, and my life is preserved" (Genesis 32:30). As we will see, the Bible speaks much of God's face and the reality of this spiritual experience in our lives.

The New Testament explains that God's presence and glory have now been revealed fully in the face, or the person, of Jesus Christ (2 Corinthians 4:6). "He is the image of the invisible God" (Colossians 1:15), the full revelation of God's person and heart. Christ is the fullness of God, revealed to humanity to bring reconciliation and peace, that we might know God.

Someday, all the perplexities and pain we encounter while living in this fallen world will be over. The Bible says, "For now we see in a mirror, dimly, but then face to face" (1 Corinthians 13:12). On this side of eternity, God has created us to know Him intimately, even though there are limitations. Someday, all the hindrances and earthly barriers will be gone and we will realize our ultimate face-to-face encounter—eternity in His holy presence.

An Intimate Encounter

God's face really speaks of His intimate, manifest presence. I like to speak of the teaching about God's presence as His *general* presence, His *indwelling* presence, and His *intimate* presence. Psalm 139 speaks of His general, invisible presence in this world. While unseen, He is present everywhere.

In the Old Testament, certain prophets, priests, and kings would know His indwelling presence, empowering them to serve, lead, speak, and pen Scripture. That presence could and would be lost due to sin. After Pentecost (Acts 2), all true believers enjoyed the indwelling presence of God because of the power of the finished work of Christ in redeeming and sanctifying human hearts. We are now sealed by the Holy Spirit with that presence until the day of our final redemption from this world (Ephesians 4:30).

> It is not about rehearsing a quick list of needs with God, but seeking Him because of who He is, with a passion for a deeper intimacy and experience of His presence.

Yet God calls us to an intimate encounter as we pursue Him with all our hearts. In my understanding, to seek His face today means to set our hearts to seek Him in worship with biblical understanding, submitting completely to the control of His Spirit with a longing to know and enjoy Him more. Again, it is not about rehearsing a quick list of needs with God, but seeking Him because of who He is, with a passion for a deeper intimacy and experience of His presence.

Paul spoke of his desire not just to "be a Christian," but also to know Him more intimately (Philippians 3:10). He prayed for this kind of intimacy for the Ephesian believers, asking that they would have a "spirit of wisdom and revelation" in order to know Christ more and to experience the "exceeding greatness of His power" (Ephesians 1:17–20). He prayed similarly for the followers in Colossae, that they would be ever "increasing in the knowledge of God" and grow in their experience of His power (Colossians 1:10–11). This would be the fruit of a commitment to seek God's face.

Other New Testament texts tell us to worship Him in "spirit and truth" (John 4:24), "abide" in intimate connection with Christ (John 15:4), and to "grow in the grace and knowledge of our Lord and Savior Jesus Christ" (2 Peter 3:18). When we seek His face, we do all of these things. In fact, none of these is ultimately accomplished if we fail to seek His face.

The Original Facebook

Facebook was founded by Mark Zuckerberg, a former Harvard student, in 2004. Initially, the membership was restricted to students at Ivy League universities but soon spread to other colleges and high schools. In 2006, it became available to anyone thirteen or older. As I write, the company says over five hundred million people are active Facebook users.

To me it is interesting that Facebook is not called Handbook, Backbook, or Footbook. The popularity of this site reminds me of our great desire to connect with a face that represents the life of a good friend, a work associate, or an acquaintance from days gone by. In fact, I really dislike it when Facebook members put some generic image or obscure picture on their profile page. I want to see a face, leading to an informed and authentic connection.

The original "Facebook" is the Bible. We see various pictures in many places of people desiring intimate connection with God's face. We also see their angst when something prevents them from experiencing the intimacy and benefits of His face.

The Old Testament followers spoke of God "hiding His face" or even setting His face against people. This reflected those times when His intimate presence and favor was hindered because of sin (Deuteronomy 32:20; Job 34:29; Psalm 13:1; 30:7; 143:7; Isaiah 54:8; Jeremiah 33:5; Ezekiel 39:23–24; Micah 3:4).

The writers of the Psalms prayed earnestly during those times when God's face was hidden. These were seasons of great distress. They felt fear of being overtaken by their enemies (Psalm 13:1–2), emotionally troubled, and even close to death (104:29; 143:7). As a result, the writers cried out for a restoration of intimacy and favor.

Psalm 80 reflects a time of God's chastisement of His people. Three times we find the prayer: "Restore us, O (Lord) God (of hosts); cause Your face to shine, and we shall be saved!" (vv. 3, 7, 19). God's face was the lifeline to these followers. Without that intimacy and blessing, they were doomed.

First Peter 3:12 says, "For the eyes of the Lord are on the righteous, and His ears are open to their prayers; but the face of the Lord is against those who do evil." Clearly we understand that intimacy with God means life and blessing. For His face to be withdrawn or set against someone (Psalm 34:16) is misery of the worst kind.

> *Intimacy with God means life and blessing. For His face to be withdrawn or set against someone (Psalm 34:16) is misery of the worst kind.*

In 1978, pediatric researchers coined a term known as the still-face effect. Through extensive experiments, experts have discovered that the normal feedback infants receive from their mothers in face-to-face interaction is distorted by having the mothers face their infants but remain facially unresponsive. The negative impact of an unresponsive face was significant. The infants studied reacted with intense wariness and eventual withdrawal, demonstrating the innate need of a child for an interactive encounter with the enlivened face of a caregiving parent.[1]

Like an infant needing a mother's responsive attention and love, we are desperate for a life-giving encounter with the face of our Creator and heavenly Father.

God's Invitation

The Scriptures are clear that God desires that His people know and enjoy Him. He is ready and responsive to restore His people, if they will again seek His face. We know the familiar call of 2 Chronicles 7:14: "If My people who are called by My name will humble themselves, and pray and seek My face, and turn from their wicked ways, then I will hear from heaven, and will forgive their sin and heal their land." In a similar way, God made the offer through the prophet Hosea: "I will return again to My place till they acknowledge their offense. Then they will seek My face; in their affliction they will earnestly seek Me" (Hosea 5:15).

God wants His children to know the blessing of seeking His face along with the intimacy and favor that comes with it: "Seek the Lord and His strength; seek His face evermore!" (1 Chronicles 16:11; Psalm 105:4). The blessings of seeking His face are reflected in Psalm 4:6–8: "Many people say, 'Who will show us better times?' Let your face smile on us, Lord. You have given me greater joy than those who have abundant harvests of grain and new wine. In peace I will lie down and sleep, for you alone, O Lord, will keep me safe" (NLT). Psalm 89:15–16 also reflects these blessings: "Blessed are the people who know the joyful sound! They walk, O Lord, in the light of Your countenance. In Your name they rejoice all day long."

We need His face to shine upon, bless, and envelop us—because all that we are and all that we do in obedience to His commands and commission is the overflow of intimacy and the fruit of His blessing.

Psalm 67 is a great missionary psalm reflecting on the many ways God blessed Israel so that they could be a blessing to the nations. At the source of all these blessings is this vital recognition: "God be merciful to us and bless us, and cause His face to shine upon us" (v. 1).

We need His face to shine upon, bless, and envelop us— because all that we are and all that we do in obedience to His commands and commission is the overflow of intimacy and the fruit of His blessing.

Face to Face With the Transformer

Sadly, too many times we engage in prayer with little thought for the reality that we are in the presence of the Almighty and that we are invited, even commanded, to seek His face. We can be encouraged by the examples in the Scriptures of those who clearly comprehended the meaning of being in His presence and carried the marks of a changed life from that moment on. (See appendix 2.)

Even the business world knows that nothing can replace the benefit of face-to-face interaction. As I write, we are in the midst of a devastating global recession. According to *Forbes* magazine, businesses have drastically reduced travel budgets and resorted to a greater use of technology in utilizing "virtual" meetings in order to save money. While 59 percent of executives said their use of technology-driven meetings had increased during the recession, eight out of ten expressed an overwhelming preference for face-to-face meetings with business associates. Executives report that face-to-face encounters are essential for "building deeper, more profitable bonds with clients and business partners and maintaining productive relationships with co-workers."[2] Just as a shortage of funds and reliance on virtual tools has diluted relationships in business, our shortage of time and distraction with technology has undermined our experience of His face. We miss the joy of the promised biblical transformation and countless blessings.

The Divine Invitation

There are countless stories, in Scripture and in history, of people who were blessed and changed by a face-to-face encounter with God. But this book is not about them. It is about us.

Here is the good news: The invitation to seek His face is offered to you, right now. I love the divine initiative of Psalm 27:8: "When You said, 'Seek My face,' my heart said to You, 'Your face, Lord, I will seek.' " He is saying to us, "Seek My face." Now we must hear the call—and answer.

One of the greatest expressions of God's heart is found in the well-known Aaronic blessing. It was the benediction pronounced by the priest after every morning and evening sacrifice with uplifted hands. It was also the blessing regularly pronounced at the close of all services in the synagogues. The people always responded to it with a united "Amen."

Here is what God wanted everyone to understand, from His heart to ours, every time His people worshiped:

> The Lord bless you and keep you;
> The Lord make *His face* shine upon you,
> And be gracious to you;
> The Lord lift up *His countenance* upon you,
> And give you peace.

NUMBERS 6:24–26

Face time with the Almighty was the key to blessing, protection, grace, and peace. It is still true today. Let us join our voices and say, "Amen!"

CHAPTER 5

Glowin' Moses and a Transformed You

Everything in our life finds proper value
once we have properly valued Him.
We take time for what we value.
And we behold what we love.
It is not the duty of beholding that changes us, though,
but rather the beauty of the one we behold.

KEN GIRE

I keep asking that the God of our Lord Jesus Christ,
the glorious Father, may give you the Spirit of wisdom and revelation,
so that you may know him better.

THE APOSTLE PAUL—EPHESIANS 1:17 (NIV)

When I was a boy, my parents and I would visit my older brother and his new wife in Missouri, where they attended Bible college. My fondest memory of those trips can be summarized in one word: fireflies. At dusk, no one needed to ask where I was. Chasing those flashing fluorescent-green insects captivated my imagination. Growing up in New Mexico, I had never seen those curious little neons of the night. We had loads of lizards, roadrunners, and tarantulas—but nothing that actually glowed.

In the ensuing years, I spent most of my adult life on the West Coast, where I never saw any fireflies. When we moved to the Twin Cities, my fascination was sparked once again. Even in my late forties you could find me in the evening hours of a muggy Minnesota June, risking my life among the myriad of mosquitoes, just to nab an occasional firefly. Now, living in Virginia, I still look forward to the invasion of these blazing bugs that consistently attract me to the backyard for a childhood re-adventure.

Scientists say that the luminosity of these little guys occurs when the enzyme luciferase acts on luciferin in the presence of magnesium ion, ATP (adenosine triphosphate), and oxygen to produce light.[1] Now, isn't that inspiring? Maybe not. However, there is one story of a luminous creature that stands above them all. I call it The Chronicle of Glowin' Moses. The explanation of his brightness is not technical but miraculous and captivating.

Reflecting a Holy Presence

Let us go back about thirty-five hundred years to a scene described in Exodus 34:29–35. Moses had just spent his second forty days on the holy mountain, meeting with God, receiving the Law from the Almighty. God left no doubt that He was speaking to Moses about His plans for His people and their worship. Think of the combination of a huge earthquake, a smoking volcano, and the roar of thunder—all wrapped up in one sensory experience. It was an unnerving display of God's holiness, truth, and power.

Without food and water for forty days (don't try this at home!), Moses met with God in intimate interchange and descended the mountain once again. With a second copy of the Decalogue (commonly known as the Ten Commandments) in hand, Moses arrived in camp—GLOWING! God's presence was so real that it left its mark on Moses' face. The brightness was so overwhelming that it frightened the people. Moses had to put a veil over his face. Every time he went back to meet with God, experiencing His intimate presence and receiving His truth for the people, Moses would remove the veil in unhindered divine fellowship. Moses knew the glory of God's presence, open-faced—only to return to speak to the people with the protection of the veil.

Matt Redman writes, "That passage gives us insight into two things: the deep revelation of God, and the change it brings to those who experience it. The greater the revelation, the greater the transformation. Unveiled in his worship and given incredible access to the presence of God, Moses also became a changed worshipper who glowed with the glory of God."[2]

Our Taste of the Glory

Call my family twisted, but one of our favorite movies is *Nacho Libre*. If you hang out with us for long you will find us quoting *Nacho Libre* lines with a cheesy Spanish accent. It is a clean comedy about a Catholic friar who is responsible for the food in a Mexican orphanage. Since childhood, Nacho has dreamed of being a famous wrestler, but it is against his religion to pursue fame and fortune through vanity and violence. He converges his dream for fame in the ring with his desire to provide better food for the children through the money from his winnings.

> "The greater the revelation, the greater the transformation."

To enter the fights, he needs a tag-team partner. In a scene early in the movie, he accosts a skinny street guy named Stephen, who had previously stolen the chips Nacho had collected for the orphans. In seeking to persuade Stephen to be his partner, Nacho urges, "Aren't you tired of getting dirt kicked in your face? Don't you want a taste of the glory? See what it tastes like?"

Stephen concedes, and the rest of the movie is a hilarious journey of two ragtag wrestlers seeking the glory and the riches of the wrestling ring. All the while, Nacho carefully conceals his exploits from the nuns, priests, and children at the orphanage using his cheap but colorful *Nacho Libre* costume. The movie ends, predictably, with Nacho winning the champion fight, collecting the big bucks, providing abundantly for the orphans, and capturing the heart of the beautiful nun.

Sometimes I get tired of the devil kicking dirt in my face when it comes to my Christian life and my endeavors in prayer. I want a taste of the glory—but not my glory. I want to taste something of what Glowin' Moses experienced.

With that inspiration in mind, stay with me because this story of Moses' glow and glory culminates in your prayer life. Let's fast-forward fifteen hundred years, from Moses to approximately AD 55. Here we find Paul comparing the scenario of Moses' Old Testament glory-glow with our own New Testament experience of the presence of Christ (2 Corinthians 3:1–4:6). Paul says that Moses' radiance was a temporary, fading exhibit of the lesser and passing power of the Law, written on stone, and ultimately bringing condemnation because of our sin. Conversely, His Spirit has called us into a new agreement with God, with truth written on our hearts, not on slabs of rock. Because of Christ, we are made righteous and now experience a glory far beyond the slow-fading glow of Moses. The glory is within us now. It is not found in a law or temple, but in the face of Jesus who invites us into an intimate encounter with himself.

> *The glory is within us now. It is not found in a law or temple, but in the face of Jesus who invites us into an intimate encounter with himself.*

At the core of this astounding presentation, Paul makes this potent declaration, "Now the Lord is the Spirit; and where the Spirit of the Lord is, there is liberty. But we all, with unveiled face, beholding as in a mirror the glory of the Lord, are being transformed into the same image from glory to glory, just as by the Spirit of the Lord. Therefore, since we have this ministry, as we have received mercy, we do not lose heart" (2 Corinthians 3:17–4:1). I urge you to read that passage again, because I believe it is the core of effective, enduring Christian ministry and the source of daily transformation.[3]

Any Moment, Any Place

These days I travel often, speaking at churches and conferences, leading prayer-energized renewal events. On the road

I am always looking to get online to accomplish my work and stay in touch with family and friends. I dislike paying for Internet access. Of course, the best connection is the free, security-enabled access—assuming someone has given me the password.

As Christians, we have free, security-enabled access to the transforming presence of God. Of course, it was costly beyond measure for Christ. Now, by His sacrifice, we enjoy free access, and the security-enabled password is *Jesus is Lord.* Again, as Paul writes, "Now the Lord is the Spirit; and where the Spirit of the Lord is, there is liberty" (2 Corinthians 3:17).

This liberty is the free, intimate, 24/7 access we have to the very Holy of Holies through our Lord Jesus Christ. We do not need a smoking mountain, a set of laws, or Moses' veil. We have all we need in the truth of Christ's redemption, the presence of His Spirit, and the invitation to seek Him at any moment and in any place.

All Inclusive!

Early in our marriage, Rosemary and I bought a time-share vacation week. Although we immediately had buyer's remorse after caving in to the high-pressured sales presentation, we have actually enjoyed it over the years, trading our week for many unique and relaxing venues. We have also learned that before you trade, you need to read the fine print about a factor known as "all-inclusive." This means that for a set fee for the week, you can eat, drink, and be merry to your heart's content. For those who spend a lot of money on alcohol, I suppose it is a good deal. For us, it is a waste of money.

> *When it comes to our access to the throne of Christ's grace, there is a very positive and powerful "all-inclusive" offer.*

When it comes to our access to the throne of Christ's grace, there is a very positive and powerful "all-inclusive" offer. Paul writes, "But we all, with unveiled face, beholding as in a mirror the glory of the Lord, are being transformed" (2 Corinthians 3:18). Every believer, all inclusive, now has the privilege of "beholding" through an intimate encounter with the glory (presence and person) of Jesus Christ. We can enjoy this reality individually and collectively every time we pray.

Granted, it is like looking in a mirror—but not a modern mirror. My wife has one of those makeup mirrors with powerful magnification. It helps her finish her beautiful face to perfection. When I use the mirror, I see what looks like craters of the moon on my nose and even a little peach fuzz hanging on for dear life atop my beautiful bald head. In contrast, the mirrors of biblical times were pieces of rough polished metal. Paul's point is this: we can enjoy the life-changing gaze of prayer as we commune with our incredible Savior. In eternity, we know it will be face-to-face and, as the hymn writer says, it will be ultimate glory for us.[4]

The Power to Become

So what is the result? At the core of credible ministry, authentic faith, and life-changing spiritual communion— what do we find? Paul says that we "are being transformed into the same image from glory to glory, just as by the Spirit of the Lord" (2 Corinthians 3:18). Yes, God uses prayer to change things. Yet at the core of Paul's theology of life and ministry is this amazing truth that communion with Christ changes us! This is no superficial rearranging of the activities, approaches, and attitudes of life. This is inside-out change. Transformation.

The English pronunciation of this Greek word is *metamourfoumetha*—very similar to our idea of a metamorphosis. It is the same word used to describe the transfiguration of Christ (Matthew 17:2), and in Romans 12:2, we are similarly challenged to be "transformed by the renewing of your mind." This is a progressive, continuous change of heart and character from one level of glory to another.

We have used this word *glory* often in these pages. It really speaks of the manifestation of God's presence, in the person of

Christ. I like to describe it as the magnification of the person of Christ on the lips of His people and the manifestation of the presence of Christ in the lives of His people. To change from "glory to glory" really speaks of an ever-advancing life of Christ-centered focus and Christlike fruitfulness. This all occurs by the power of the indwelling Spirit of Christ in our lives. We are captivated by Christ, changed by Christ, and conformed to Christ.

Calvin Miller is compelling in his description of Paul's desire to be changed to the glory of Christ's image: "This is Narcissus in reverse. The poor Greek lad! He looked into a pond, saw himself, and drowned struggling to embrace his own ego. On the other hand, we look into a glass and see Jesus and are given life by our desire to become the Christ in our mirror."[5]

First Encounter!

This idea of transforming prayer was more than theory to Paul. He had been looking for glory in the Old Covenant. He was a model Pharisee, striving with all his religious might to keep the law and prove his spiritual prowess, even to the point of chasing down the newfangled fanatics known as Christians and throwing them in the slammer, or worse (see Philippians 3:4–6).

As you know, everything changed for Paul (formerly Saul) one day on the dirt road to Damascus when the living Christ appeared in radiance and drove Paul to his face. In his very first prayer response to the living Christ, Paul asked, "Who are You, Lord?" (Acts 9:5). In his second prayer, he uttered, "Lord, what do You want me to do?" (9:6). Then for three days, this blind, radically converted Jew fasted in solitude—probably experiencing the answer to his first two prayer questions.

At the same time, Christ tells a man named Ananias to go find Paul and baptize him. Reluctant because of Paul's reputation as a relentless persecutor, Ananias appeals. Jesus assures Ananias of Paul's change of heart with these simple and profound words: "Behold, he is praying" (Acts 9:11).

We do not know with certainty what Paul prayed about for those three days. We know his heart was immediately touched on that Damascus road with a desire to know Christ and His will for Paul's life. We do know that in the course of all of his writings, Paul never requested prayer for an arthritic knee, hair loss, or quick healing of his many back wounds inflicted by his persecutors. He often prayed for a greater knowledge of Jesus, a deeper joy in suffering, a fuller experience of His love, an enduring boldness in preaching Christ, and an ultimate revelation of His glory (Philippians 1:19–26; 3:10; Ephesians 3:14–19; 6:19–20).

Paul understood transforming prayer from the moment of his first encounter with Christ. He never got over it and never stopped growing in it. He saw it as the core of his credibility and the life-source of all Christian living.

Time to Go for the Glory

Fireflies are entertaining. Glowin' Moses was truly amazing. Paul was changed in a moment. Still, there is nothing so attractive and captivating in this sin-darkened world as a Christian who experiences and exhibits the glory of Jesus through the power of face-to-face intimacy.

Now it is time to begin to understand the core truths and practices that make prayer so transformational. It's time to go for the glory.

Free for Life!
A Trophy of Transformation

A dozen years ago, my friend Bob took the challenge of going away for three days to pray with a group of about eighty men from our church. It seemed crazy that busy men would take vacation time, drive a couple hours to a run-down camp, sleep on worn-out beds, eat lousy food, and do nothing but pray for three days. Yet I've seen it happen dozens of times—with life-changing results.

On the second afternoon, Bob sat with a group of about twenty-five men. The brothers all participated, as they felt prompted, through spontaneous Scripture reading, songs, and heartfelt response. The Word, the Spirit, and the prayers of the men were creating an environment of fresh spiritual hunger and unprecedented transparency. Overwhelmed by a sense of God's presence and compelled by his desperation for a breakthrough, Bob stepped to the middle of this circle of praying men, sat down in a chair, and began to weep.

With unedited brokenness, Bob confessed to God and the men listened in on this holy moment. He wept over the loss of his first marriage, recalling the departure of his wife and young daughter due to his addiction to pornography. He thanked the Lord for his subsequent salvation and marriage to a godly Christian woman. His heartache then accelerated as he confessed his ongoing secret struggle with porn. He cried out with pleas for God's forgiveness, healing, and restoration in his life.

This holy moment was not prompted by a long prayer list. It did not spring from any human pressure or peer manipulation. Bob was transformed because he took time to behold Christ's glory with an open Bible, a yielded heart, and an expectant faith.

Today, Bob is in heaven. Yet through the remaining years of his life, he walked in consistent victory. He shared his story with other men. He enjoyed healthy accountability with his Christian brothers and his wife. God used him to help others—and to draw more men to that place of transforming prayer.

PART TWO

BEST-PRACTICES
PRAYING

CHAPTER 6

The Case of the Missing Prayer List

It is possible to ask for good things for bad reasons . . .
How tragic then if our prayer for good things leaves us
still thinking of ourselves first,
still thinking of God's will primarily in terms of its immediate effect
on ourselves, still longing for blessing simply so that we will be blessed.

D. A. CARSON

Your Father knows the things you have need of
before you ask Him.

JESUS—MATTHEW 6:8

Let's talk about best practices . . . not good, not acceptable, not traditional, not comfortable, not common practices—but the best. That is the passion of this section. My prayer is that these ideas and ideals will inspire you to something very biblical, fresh, practical, and transforming in your prayer life.

Best practice—a term common to the business world—is "a technique or methodology that, through experience and research, has proven to reliably lead to a desired result. [It involves] a commitment to using . . . all the knowledge, experience, and technology at one's disposal to ensure success. The term is used frequently in the fields of health care, government administration, the education system, project management, hardware and software product development, and elsewhere."[1]

In relation to prayer, we want to use all we know from the Scriptures to discover the best practices. We want to learn to understand the leading of the Spirit to experience and achieve the desired result—the glory of God (we will talk more about this "desired result" as you continue to read). This would be "best-practices praying."

According to the American Productivity and Quality Center, "The three main barriers to adoption of a best practice are a lack of knowledge about current best practices, a lack of motivation to make changes involved in their adoption, and a lack of knowledge and skills required to do so."[2] Accordingly, we need to thoroughly know and understand what it means to seek God's face in worship-based prayer. We need the Spirit to give us holy dissatisfaction and the motivation to change. We need to know how to engage in transforming prayer.

No Prayer Leftovers

To realize best-practices prayer, we must take an honest look at where we are. Good things are taking place in the lives of many Christians. Churches are making noble attempts to pray. Yet we all want God's best, which I believe is clear in the Scriptures and within reach of every true believer.

Unfortunately, we seem to give God our spiritual leftovers in prayer. If you were celebrating your tenth wedding anniversary and wanted it to be the best it could be, you would not announce to your spouse, "We are going to stay home and have leftovers." If your son was graduating from high school, you would want to host the best party possible. You would not roll out a full spread of nondescript table scraps from last week's menu of mundane family meals.

When we engage in the great privilege and joy of prayer with a "leftovers mentality," the likelihood of spiritual blessing is slight. The Lord says, "Love me with all of your heart," worship me "in spirit and in truth," present your bodies as a "living sacrifice." He calls for our passionate best. Instead, we bring spiritual leftovers to the throne of grace. This is not a best practice. Far from it.

Quality Not Quantity

In Malachi 1, God addressed this attitude of spiritual leftovers, which had become acceptable in the worship routines of Israel. Three times a year God invited the nation to come to the Jerusalem temple and worship with the offering of their grains and animals. This was an expression of thanksgiving for God's goodness following a harvest and for the atonement of their sins. The Lord did not require great quantities—but He did ask for their first and best as a demonstration of their gratitude to God as the source of all their blessings and an indication of their reverence for God as the One worthy of worship.

Instead, they were bringing leftovers. They offered blind, lame, and sick animals at the temple. Because the thoughtfulness and quality of the gift represented the value of the one to whom they were giving it, this became a serious spiritual failure. God notes that they would not give these kinds of thoughtless, shallow, and flawed offerings to their fathers or their governor, yet they were bringing them to God. The priests were conducting good services. The people were going through the motions. On the surface, all looked well.

He calls for our passionate best. Instead, we bring spiritual leftovers to the throne of grace. This is not a best practice. Far from it.

Yet in Malachi 1:6 we find, " 'Where is My honor? And if I am a Master, where is My reverence?' says the Lord of hosts to you priests who despise My name." God then reiterates His ultimate concern: "'I have no pleasure in you . . . nor will I accept an offering from your hands. For from the rising of the sun, even to its going down, My name shall be great among the Gentiles; in every place incense shall be offered to My name, and a pure offering; for My name shall be great among the nations . . . for I am a great King,' says the Lord of hosts, 'and My name is to be feared among the nations'" (Malachi 1:10–11, 14).

Acceptable Sacrifices

Today, we are far removed from that scene in Jerusalem. Christ has become our atoning sacrifice, so we no longer need animals or grain. Yet our gratitude to and reverence for God in prayer and worship should continue. As it says in 1 Peter 2:4–5, "Coming to Him as to a living stone, rejected indeed by men, but chosen by God and precious, you also, as living stones, are being built up a spiritual house, a holy priesthood, to offer up spiritual sacrifices acceptable to God through Jesus Christ." Did you catch that? "*Sacrifices acceptable to God* through Jesus Christ." Even today, not all sacrifices are created equal.

From a New Testament standpoint, acceptable sacrifices include:

- A commitment to worship in spirit and in truth (John 4:22–24)
- A genuine sacrifice of praise, giving thanks to His name (Hebrews 13:15)
- The presentation of our bodies in complete surrender (Romans 12:1–2)
- A life of love that produces right living (Philippians 1:9–11)
- Doing everything "in the name of the Lord Jesus" with thanksgiving (Colossians 3:17)
- Service conducted in supernatural power (1 Peter 4:11)
- Generosity that flows from a heart of love (Philippians 4:10–19)

Relating to prayer, God is not looking for a dutiful contribution of time or energy in the spirit of religious observance. He is looking for a hungry heart that seeks after Him in praise, gratitude, and loving surrender, with a readiness to pray, think, and live like Jesus as the expression and overflow of that intimacy.

I fear sometimes that our routine and dutiful approach to prayer may be missing the mark of God's heart and concern for

His own glory. We must continue to grow so that we understand prayer as more of a transforming experience in the Holy of Holies and less like a rushed trip to the grocery store to grab what we think we need for the day.

The Case of the Misguided Prayer List

Not long ago, I conducted a renewal weekend at a large evangelical church in the Rocky Mountain region. During those days, one of the staff members approached me with some fascinating information. Among his duties was direct oversight of the prayer efforts of the church. He had conducted a study of the prayer requests made known during their adult Sunday school classes and then published the results with some insightful commentary.

As the following graphic shows, he divided the requests into seven categories. Most of the categories were self-explanatory, but a couple of them needed clarification. Events/Happenings included things like prayer for a job interview, kids starting school, safe travel to Dallas, work not going so well, etc. "Unspoken" Requests encompassed general requests for prayer for an issue or situation without giving any details.

Adult Sunday School Prayer Requests (by category)

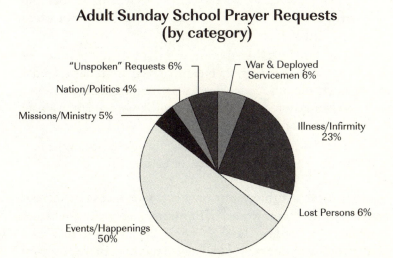

"Unspoken" Requests 6%
Nation/Politics 4%
Missions/Ministry 5%
War & Deployed Servicemen 6%
Illness/Infirmity 23%
Lost Persons 6%
Events/Happenings 50%

In a message sent to the Sunday school leaders, the staff pastor commented:

This is far from a scientific survey. However, I do think it gives us some insight into our prayer times. Here are some of my observations:

- I was surprised that Illness/Infirmity was not the highest. I'm not sure if we are just a healthier church or if we just have a lot of things going on that eclipse this category.
- Prayer for Lost Persons averaged one lost person for every two [Sunday school] classes. Should we wonder why baptisms are at a five-year low in our church? I think the problem is that we do not place enough priority on praying for the lost.
- I expected prayer for Missions/Ministry to be higher. As missions-minded as our church is, I expected to see more prayer in this area. This could have just been a bad week for this.
- I was shocked at the disproportionate number of requests for Events/Happenings. First, let me say that I do not think there is any need that is too small or trivial to bring to God. What shocks me is the overwhelming focus on requests for things WE are doing, events WE are involved in, stuff WE are dealing with, etc.
- The ratio looks like this: One prayer for a lost person, one prayer for missions, then eight prayers from our calendar and to-do list. Again, please understand that God wants us to bring all requests to Him. I think we need to evaluate the ratio of our prayer content.
- There was not one single prayer for revival or awakening in our church, community, or nation. Sad.

As I surveyed the results of this prayer snapshot, my gut reaction is that this is typical of the average prayer list, whether compiled in a Sunday school class or a personal journal. Thank God, people *are* praying, yet I believe something more powerful and purposeful can be discovered about the reality of prayer. No one really wants to serve God leftovers.

Rethinking Our Lists

I have to admit, I have never been much of a prayer-list person. Maybe this is because I tend to be spontaneous—even borderline ADD. Perhaps I am just not organized or disciplined enough to keep up with all the details. Frankly, I admire those who manage long lists of needs, answers, commentary, and details. I found that I was spending more time organizing, rewriting, or trying to find my list than I was actually spending time in prayer.

For some people, lists and guides can be very helpful. In fact, our ministry promotes a classic prayer tool called *The 29:59 Plan*, which was created by one of my mentors, Peter Lord. He designed it in the mid-seventies to help the people of his church pray thirty minutes a day, but in a non-legalistic way (thus the idea of 29 minutes and 59 seconds). As far as tools go—this is my favorite because it helps me keep a balanced approach to the many areas that merit my prayer attention. It also contains some fabulous sections of Scripture-based prayers of praise and adoration so that all requests are guided by biblical truth and God-ward priorities.[3]

Lists can help us remember things for which we should pray. They help us track answers to prayer. They can help us remember details like names, ministry issues, dates, and elements of spiritual progress in situations and lives. Lists can prevent our minds from wandering in prayer. Perhaps when it comes to journaling and managing lists we are safe to conclude "to each his own."

Yet in group settings, the focus on lists of needs and prolonged discussions about details can distract from the purpose. Some groups spend significant time talking and taking notes about issues, people, and problems. This has two effects. First, a gathering that was announced as a prayer meeting becomes mostly a discussion session. At times, those discussions border on gossip. This is not a best practice.

Second, we can tend to be operating simply in the realm of our own human thoughts, our own observations, and our own ideas about what we should pray about. We often ask the question, "What do we need to pray about?" This is followed by long discussion of detailed situations in our lives, the lives of others, the church, community, and society. Sometimes the discussion occurs as if the Lord was not even in the room, aware of the problems, or had any opinion about the subjects at hand.

What's the Big Deal?

So you are probably thinking, *Come on, Henderson, what's the big deal? At least folks are trying to keep track of things in their prayer lives! Be grateful people are getting together to pray.* Yes, praise God for faithful praying people. However, this section is about best-practices praying—and we all know that being stuck in a rut of practicing good things can become a hindrance to the practice of the best things.

Someone might ask, "Aren't we supposed to bear one another's burdens?" (Galatians 6:2). Yes, and praying for someone can be a part of that ministry. However, too many of us use prayer as an excuse to avoid the inconvenience of actually bearing the burden. Picking someone's name off a list and tossing up a perfunctory prayer is sometimes a replacement for the real work of sacrificing time and energy to serve. The idea of bearing one another's burdens literally implies "taking something up with the hands" or to physically carry their load. Prayer is vital—but we must roll up our sleeves at times and watch a young mother's children while she is at the doctor, clean her house once a week, or actually give time, funds, or labor needed in a moment of hardship.

Now, I do not want to offend or anger anyone by what I am about to say, but I have to put it on the table: I find little evidence in the Bible for our routine emphasis on extensive prayer lists focused almost entirely on temporal concerns.[4] I do not want to be legalistic here. But I do want to jolt us out of a rut of thinking that lists are the key to effective prayers.

Lists are simply tools. It is important to keep in mind that, in any arena of the Christian life, tools are meant to be used for a greater purpose, not cherished as *the* greater purpose. Lists, if used at all, must remain as servants and not revered as masters.

I am not suggesting that everyone stop using prayer lists. But we must recognize the possibility that our prayer lists are replacing the Scriptures and the Spirit as the primary content providers for our prayer times. We want to keep pursuing best practices that meet the goal of God's glory. Again, we must embrace prayer as transformational, not merely utilitarian.

> *Lists are simply tools. It is important to keep in mind that, in any arena of the Christian life, tools are meant to be used for a greater purpose, not cherished as* the *greater purpose.*

Awakened From a Spiritual Coma:
A Trophy of Transformation

Sharon and her husband, Dale, own a service business specializing in information technology. For most of her Christian life, Sharon struggled with insecurity and feelings of unworthiness. She had a hard time really comprehending and experiencing the love of Christ. As a result she struggled with her weight, worked hard to be accepted, and never really sensed the deep well-being that came from authentic intimacy.

Several years ago, she was introduced to worship-based prayer. As she learned more about the power of seeking God's face, not just His hand, she began to taste the power of transformation. "The need to perform to be accepted became a thing of the past. The Lord began to awaken my heart from its spiritually comatose state. I have found freedom and healing that I never thought possible. My life is completely different, as I've come to know, really know, that God loves me. I see myself the way He sees me, forgiven and free to experience Him."

As is always the case, this transforming grace leads to the desire to share Christ's life with others. Sharon subsequently went on two overseas mission trips to Peru and Kenya. She received training as a disaster responder in order to meet the needs of people in crisis. After the devastating earthquake that hit Haiti in early 2010, she deployed as a voluntary chaplain.

Now, as worship-based prayer has become a lifestyle in her personal walk with Christ, Sharon continues to flourish with a confidence and well-being that allows her to focus on the needs of others. "I've searched all my life for love and often in the wrong places. But those days are behind me. I've gone from being someone who was very concerned about what people thought of me, to a person whom God has and is changing on the inside and who cares only that I am surrendered and pleasing to Him."

CHAPTER 7

All Prayer Requests Are Not Created Equal

*We spend more prayer energy
trying to keep sick Christians out of heaven
than trying to keep lost people out of hell.*

JAMES WALKER

*You ask and do not receive,
because you ask amiss,
that you may spend it on your pleasures.*

JAMES 4:3

Asking is a vital component of our relationship with God. This is true because He has commanded us to seek Him as our ultimate source in all things. He has ordained prayer as the means by which we depend on and trust in Him. He answers our prayers to give us what He knows we need to bring Him glory.

Yet in today's Western culture, permanently infected with materialism and a consumer mindset, it is sometimes difficult for Christians to ask for things from God without a fundamentally selfish aspiration and a chronic aversion to suffering in any form. We often pray to escape our difficulties rather than embrace discipleship.

Like anyone, I love it when God answers my prayers in ways that make my life more pleasant or pain-free. Yet I am learning that my deepest needs are met when my heart is most closely aligned with the Word of God, the Son of God, the Spirit of God, and the purposes of God. I feel God calling me, and many others I know, beyond superficial solutions as the focus of our prayers. Asking is the doorway, not just to getting our next lunch ticket or luxury item but to discovering the profound joy of a transformed life.

> *It is so easy to reduce our focus in prayer to the typical "organ recital" concerns about Paula's pancreas, Larry's liver, Sarah's stomach, and Artie's appendix.*

I am so grateful the Father cares about every detail of my life. He even counts the number of hairs on my head, which does not take as long for me as it does for the average person. Yet, it is so easy to reduce our focus in prayer to the typical "organ recital" concerns about Paula's pancreas, Larry's liver, Sarah's stomach, and Artie's appendix. Our Father knows, cares, and is fully capable of taking care of all these needs according to His will and glory. Yet the privilege of prayer offers so much more.

Birds, Lilies, and the Kingdom

In the Sermon on the Mount, we find some of the more familiar commands to trust God for His provision. In His hillside discourse, Jesus tells what it means to live according to His kingdom principles rather than the world's values or the self-righteous systems of the Pharisees. We all love the beauty of the Beatitudes. We know that in Matthew, chapter 6, Jesus preaches the importance of pure motives in our giving, praying, and fasting. He warns against materialism. He provides a powerful antidote for worry by illustrating His care for the birds of the sky and the flowers of the field. With His unique authority and assurance, He delivers the command, "But seek first the kingdom of God and His righteousness, and all these things shall be added to you" (v. 33).

In considering these truths, we must search our souls about the things that trigger our prayers. What values shape our requests? Are our motives honoring to Christ? To what degree are "earthly treasures" and the "god of mammon" infecting our prayer life? Amid all our worries about our health, finances, family, job, education, and ministry concerns, are we seeking first His kingdom and not our own?

Good God

In Matthew 7:7–8, Jesus urges, "Ask, and it will be given to you; seek, and you will find; knock, and it will be opened to you. For everyone who asks receives, and he who seeks finds, and to him who knocks it will be opened." He reminds us that just as earthly fathers know how to give good things to their children, so our heavenly Father knows how to give good things to those who ask.

What might Jesus have in mind with His commands to ask, seek, and knock? A pay raise? A new car? An all-expenses-paid vacation? What are the good things He promises? In the context, Jesus spoke specifically of the basic provisions of bread and fish, with no mention of fishing boats, lake cabins, or new video games. Perhaps the answer is in the point He has already made, that the truly "good" things we seek first are the issues pertaining to the kingdom of God.

In a parallel passage found in Luke's gospel, Jesus clarifies His focus on the good things we should expect with these words: "How much more will your heavenly Father give the Holy Spirit to those who ask Him!" (Luke 11:13). The life spring of all the good things the Father wants to give us is the presence and power of the Holy Spirit.

Clearly, these teachings, like other instructions about prayer, are not carte blanche encouragements to concoct a long list of anything our heart desires. Rather, it is a promise of basic provision, spiritual empowerment, and guidance for His kingdom purposes.

Toward Spontaneity and Substance

Two vital concerns emerge here. First is the need to allow the good gift of the Spirit to lead us in the freedom to pray His heart, not our predetermined ideas. The second issue is the need to align our attitude and approach with the patterns of the Scriptures when we are praying about issues and needs. God continues to teach me so many amazing lessons about the need for spiritual spontaneity over routine rehearsals of prayer lists. He keeps calling me to align my prayers more completely with the precepts, priorities, and patterns of Scripture.

A. W. Tozer, with his typically prophetic and profound insight, spoke of the need for a fresh, Spirit-guided approach to the Christian life in his essay "Beware the File-Card Mentality:" "The essence of true religion is spontaneity, the sovereign moving of the Holy Spirit upon and in the free spirit of redeemed men. This has through the years of human history been the hallmark of spiritual excellence, the evidence of reality in a world of unreality." Tozer went on to note that when our faith "loses its sovereign character and becomes mere form, this spontaneity is lost also, and in its place come precedence, propriety, system . . . the belief that spirituality can be organized . . . numbers, statistics, the law of averages, and other such natural human things. And creeping death always follows."[1]

> *"The essence of true religion is spontaneity, the sovereign moving of the Holy Spirit upon and in the free spirit of redeemed men."*

Tozer noted that our need for organization and structure "is a good thing in its place and deadly out of its place. Its danger comes from the well-known human tendency to depend upon external helps in dealing with internal things." Then he delivered this riveting warning: "Nothing but an internal spiritual revolution can deliver the victim from his fate."[2]

Regarding prayer, Tozer spoke boldly about the person who becomes restricted to external forms rather than responsive to the Spirit:

> *His prayers lose their freedom and become less spontaneous, less effective. He finds himself concerned over matters that should give him no concern whatever—how much time he*

spent in prayer yesterday, whether he did or did not cover his prayer list for the day, whether he gets up as early as he used to do or stay up in prayer as late at night. Inevitably, the calendar crowds out the Spirit and the face of the clock hides the face of God. Prayer ceases to be the free breath of a ransomed soul and becomes a duty to be fulfilled. And even if under such circumstances he succeeds in making his prayer amount to something, still he is suffering tragic losses and binding upon his soul a yoke from which Christ died to set him free.[3]

> "Inevitably, the calendar crowds out the Spirit and the face of the clock hides the face of God. Prayer ceases to be the free breath of a ransomed soul and becomes a duty to be fulfilled."

Comparing the Content

We know we are supposed to bring our requests to God. Yet one of the most important questions we need to ask is how the content of our prayers differ from the biblical patterns and teaching about the things we should be praying about. I would suggest that the prayer requests we find in the Bible are shorter, deeper, and fundamentally different in nature than the lists that can tend to dominate the prayer approach of modern Christians.

Praying Just Like Jesus?

Scripture records numerous examples of Jesus' prayer life. We find six references to Jesus' prayers that give no clear indication of the content of what He said (Mark 1:35; 6:46; Luke 3:21; 9:18, 28; 11:1). We find He often withdrew from activity in order to enjoy private communion with the Father. While we do not know the substance of His prayers in these times, it appears they were directly related to fresh empowerment for His self-less, sacrificial service. There are also occasions where Jesus blesses people, but His exact words are not given (Mark 10:16; Luke 24:50).

In the final part of this book we will look at the model prayer Jesus gave His disciples as a primary pattern for transforming prayer (Matthew 6:9–13; Luke 11:2–4). We do find other brief accounts of Jesus' prayer life and the themes that shaped His spoken prayers. Appendix 3 lists Jesus' specific prayers. In summary, His prayer life was distinguished by intimate expressions of worship, thanksgiving, surrender, and gracious intercession for the faith of others.

Many modern-day teachers encourage us to "do" like Jesus, lead like Jesus, and speak like Jesus. Our passion must also be to embrace these truths so we can pray like Jesus.

Redirected Disciples

During Jesus' earthly ministry, the disciples were in constant physical interaction with Him, so in many ways, their very conversations were prayers. When it came to specific instances of prayer, they admitted their desire and need to learn (Luke 11:1). Typically, their prayers were selfish and sleepy. They jockeyed for prominence in their requests to Jesus, wanted to call down fire on those who rejected their message, and often doubted.

However, after the Spirit came to permanently indwell them at Pentecost, their prayers changed. John Franklin describes it: "They went from being on their own agenda to being on God's agenda. They quit seeking a seat on Jesus' right and His left and began praying for boldness to testify in the face of persecution. They quit flirting with a return to fishing and focused on shepherding the people of God. They stopped worrying about their circumstances and began seeking an endowment of power from on high to preach the gospel. They changed from being self-centered to being God-centered. This determined their power with God—or rather His power through them."[4]

We see the early church in prayer most often seeking the advancement of the gospel through any circumstance. They prayed daily as part of a vital regimen of spiritual growth—for the sake of the gospel (Acts 2:42). In the face of attack, they gathered to pray from the Scriptures, requesting fresh power for boldness—for the sake of the gospel (Acts 4:31). When they were persecuted, they rejoiced in God for the honor of suffering—for the sake of the gospel—rather than asking for a reprieve (Acts 5:41). When Peter was in jail, they prayed for his release—for the sake of the gospel (Act 12:5). When Paul and Silas were in jail, they rejoiced in prayer and singing, trusting God—for the sake of the gospel (Acts 16:25).

Paul's Prayer Points

The New Testament also contains the specific prayers of the apostle Paul, offered as he wrote his inspired letters. This is our best snapshot of his prayer lists. In summary, we see this:

- 1 Thessalonians 3:9–13—Paul asks God to make a way for him to see the Thessalonian believers again in order to build up their faith. He prays for an increase and overflow of their love and prays that their hearts would be strengthened toward a greater holiness in light of the return of Christ.
- 2 Thessalonians 1:3–12—Paul offers thanksgiving for the faith, love, and perseverance of the Thessalonians in the midst of trials, trusting in God's justice to reward the godly and punish the ungodly. He prays that God would fulfill His purposes in them, that the name of the Lord Jesus would be glorified in them by grace, and that their ultimate glorification (perfection) would be realized.
- Ephesians 1:3–23—After giving great praise to God for our blessings in Christ, God's sovereignty in our salvation, the abundance of Christ's grace, the reign of Christ and our guaranteed inheritance through the Holy Spirit, Paul prays for the Ephesian believers. In this prayer (vv. 15–23), he prays that the Spirit would allow them to know Christ more, that they would know the hope of their inheritance, and that they would experience the fullness of His power working in them.
- Ephesians 3:14–21—Paul again bows his knee to the Father, thankful that through the mystery of Christ the entire family of God (both Jew and Gentile) has been

named. Then he prays that they might be strengthened by the power of the Holy Spirit in their inner man. Next, he desires that the Ephesians might grasp the limitless vastness of Christ's unsurpassed love. Paul concludes with the passionate cry of benediction to the One who does exceedingly abundantly above what we can imagine, that to Him will be glory in the church forever and ever.

- Philippians 1:3–11—After expressing thanks to God for the Philippians because of his affection for them and their vital partnership with him in the work of the gospel, he requests that their love would abound, based on their knowledge of truth. He then asks that they would have discernment to do the best things and that they would become blameless until the day of Christ. He also prays that they will live out the righteousness of Christ for the glory of God.
- Colossians 1:3–14—Again, Paul begins this flow of prayer with thanksgiving for their genuine belief in the gospel as evidenced in their faith, love, and hope. He then references his nonstop prayers on their behalf, asking God to fill them with the knowledge of His will so they will walk worthy of Christ, pleasing Him, and bearing spiritual fruit. He prays for an increasing knowledge of God, strength to endure, and a spirit of joyful thanksgiving. The prayer moves immediately back into worship of the uniqueness of Christ and the power of His redeeming work.

Every one of Paul's model prayers sprang from expressions of thanksgiving, truths about God, and notes of praise. They are the fruit of his worship and intimate, experiential knowledge of the person of Christ. Paul's requests were focused on the growing faith and love of believers with the goal of God's glory.

Our Requests vs. Paul's Requests

In our day, we have become accustomed to requesting prayer for virtually every possible subject. Sometimes the details are very missional, sometimes mundane. I am reminded of the story of a young boy who was misbehaving during the morning worship service. The parents did their best to control him but were losing the battle. Finally the father picked up the little fellow and walked out to apply some firm correction. Just before reaching the foyer, the boy called out loudly to the congregation: "Pray for me! Pray for me!"

In another church, in the Ozarks, a sweet elderly lady requested prayer during a Sunday service for her husband's upcoming surgery. She announced, "Pray for Harold. They're gonna do surgery and remove his prostitute." The congregation roared, the pastor was dumbfounded, and the service never got back on track.

In light of our sometimes significant, sometimes silly patterns, we should look to the Bible to review the occasions when Paul asked for prayer. This can also give us some vital guidance about our own requests for prayer. A review of Paul's specific personal prayer requests (see appendix 4) reveals a consistent focus on the advancement of the Gospel message, the fulfillment of the mission, and the ultimate glory of God in all things.

What's on Your Prayer List?

Perhaps the fundamental difference between our prayer lists and the prayer concerns we find in the Bible is that we pray about personal problems, while most of the biblical prayers focus on Christ's purposes. Worship-based prayers set the foundation for something other than "me" prayers, because they start with a "Thee" focus. This changes the nature of how we pray.

The fundamental difference between our prayer lists and the prayer concerns we find in the Bible is that we pray about personal problems, while most of the biblical prayers focus on Christ's purposes.

D. A. Carson, in his outstanding book *A Call to Spiritual Reformation: Priorities from Paul and His Prayers*, presents a powerful inquiry that should motivate us to evaluate the nature of our prayer lists:

We must ask ourselves how far the petitions we commonly present to God are in line with what Paul prays for. Suppose, for example, that 80 or 90 percent of our petitions ask God for good health, recovery from illness, safety on the road, a good job, success in exams, the emotional needs of our children, success in our mortgage application, and much more of the same. How much of Paul's praying revolves around equivalent items? If the center of our praying is far removed from the center of Paul's praying, then even our very praying may serve as a wretched testimony to the remarkable success of the processes of paganization in our life and thought.[5]

Strong words, indeed. Yet they are a necessary wake-up call as we look at the values, aspirations, and longings that drive our prayers.

Lord, teach us to pray.

CHAPTER 8

Go for the Glory!

The glory of the Father must be the aim and end,
the very soul and life of our prayer.

ANDREW MURRAY

Not unto us, O Lord, not unto us,
but to Your name give glory.

PSALM 115:1

The *Westminster Shorter Catechism* declares: "A man's chief end is to *glorify* God, and to enjoy him forever." If this ideal captures the very purpose of our existence, certainly prayer, that most intimate connection by which we enjoy God, must also exist for His glory.

Prayer becomes transformational when we embrace the original and enduring context for all praying. A worship-based approach fixes our heart first on the majesty of God, the person of Christ, the purity of His Word—and excites within us an appetite for Him. Our very motives for prayer are changed and elevated beyond anything merely earthly. Our heart is renewed with a longing for His glory.

Let God Be Magnified

I'll never forget Bill Sheehan. He was a long-time member of the church I attended while in college. A respected deacon, Bill was notable as a mighty man of prayer. I joined Bill on a few occasions in the prayer chapel at the church. Indeed, he understood the priority and power of prayer. You knew it when he prayed.

The pastor would often call on Bill to pray in the church services, typically before the offering. I recall that Bill's prayers were potent and passionate—but not very long or complicated. The most memorable characteristic of this seasoned prayer warrior's approach was that prior to any prayer, he declared, "Let God be magnified!"

As a college student, I found Bill's prayer routine a bit quirky. I understood later that his reason for this animated declaration was rooted in the admonition of Psalm 70:4, where it says, "Let all those who seek You rejoice and be glad in You; and let those who love Your salvation say continually, 'Let God be magnified!'"

I am convinced Bill's peculiar opening line defined something powerful he understood about prayer. It was a mark of the maturity of his relationship with God and the effectiveness of his prayer life. Psalm 70:4 had taught Bill that prayer is about seeking God, rejoicing in Him, and continually focusing on His glory. Yes, let God be magnified!

Suntan Lotion in a Snowstorm

Unlike Bill Sheehan, many of us fail to focus our prayers on the core motive: that God would be magnified in everything we seek or say. If we were to be honest, our prayers are often motivated by a desire for comfort and convenience. Many times our prayers are viewed as a divinely ordained way to get what we want out of life, or to avoid what we don't want. It is easy to fall into the trap of thinking prayer exists so God can be used to help us preserve our glory rather than our being used to promote His glory.

Pastor and author John Piper puts it in proper perspective when he writes:

> *God's goal at every stage of creation and salvation is to magnify His glory. You can magnify with a microscope or with a telescope. A microscope magnifies by making tiny things look bigger than they are. A telescope magnifies by making gigantic things (like stars), look tiny, appear more as they really are. God designed the universe to magnify the glory of His grace the way a telescope magnifies the stars. Everything He does in our salvation is designed to magnify the glory of his grace like this.*[1]

I wonder if sometimes our worry about our requests and problems is not more like the microscope that takes tiny things and magnifies them out of proportion. We need the telescope to take God's glory and make it the delight and fabric of our praying and living.

We pray, perhaps sincerely, but dramatically out of context; like applying suntan lotion in a snowstorm, wearing a heavy down jacket on a tropical cruise, or singing "The Star Spangled Banner" on a busy street corner in Tehran, Iran. Our prayers often are a misfit in light of the real purpose and context of prayer. We may be genuine but we risk being genuinely misguided.

When we understand the ultimate reason for prayer, our asking is no longer aimless. Our "crying out" has deeper conviction. Our prayers for miracles rise fervently because we know God can heal, or heal us of the desire to be healed—all for His glory. Our intercession looks beyond temporal needs and targets transcendent realities that have eternal significance, for His glory.

What Motivates God?

I remember reading in a devotional book some years ago that the only thing that motivates God is His own glory. To our tiny minds that may sound egotistical, but we must remember that God is the Creator and the One to whom glory is due in the purity and beauty of His holiness. He deserves it.

> The only thing that motivates God is His own glory.

I am motivated by so many lesser things, even in my prayer life: perhaps especially in my prayer life. God's glory should be our sole—and soul—motivation that frames and filters everything we pray. John Piper reiterated, "The chief end of man is to *glorify* God and enjoy Him forever. And the chief act of man by which the unity of these two goals is preserved is prayer."[2]

In John 14:13, Jesus gave us a standard for all of our praying, "And whatever you ask in My name, that I will do, that the Father may be *glorified* in the Son." What motivates us to ask can often be all over the map. What motivates our Father to answer is that He would be *glorified* in our prayers through the person and work of His Son, Jesus Christ. Jonathan Edwards, the great Puritan preacher and author, wrote, "It appears that all that is ever spoken of in the Scriptures as an ultimate end of God's works is included in that one phrase, 'the glory of God.'"[3]

Christ's Work in Us for His Glory

No one ever lived with more passion and intentionality than Jesus, our Master and model. Everything in His life was for the glory of the Father (John 11:4; 13:31–31; 17:1, 4–5). He is our ultimate example for everything we do, including our prayers.

The ultimate result of God's salvation plan is that every knee should bow and every tongue should confess "that Jesus Christ is Lord, to the *glory* of God the Father" (Philippians 2:10–11). Jesus came, lived, loved, served, sacrificed, died, and rose again—for God's glory.

Prayer is the core of our relationship with Christ. This relationship into which we have been called, through the grace of Jesus, exists for God's glory. Christ has saved us for God's glory and is setting us apart to himself for His glory.

In life's journey we learn, we mature, we serve, we grow—through the good times and the bad—all for His glory. Meanwhile, we pray in passionate worship, surrender, and trust. Our prayers are an intricate and essential part of His glory. With fresh conviction and passion we can embrace the truth of 1 Corinthians 10:31, where it tells us, "Whether you eat or drink, or whatever you do [including prayer]—do all to the *glory* of God." (See appendix 5 for additional Scripture references to God's glory.)

An Agonizing Alignment

Inspiring as these reminders are, our flesh struggles to pray in alignment with the truth of God's glory. Our prayer lists can easily become so saturated with our desires for ease, comfort, convenience, and accomplishment, that the goal of God's glory becomes obscured. Our human tendency to avoid pain, loss, and difficulty can dilute our passion for God's glory. When our goals and God's glory are in conflict, it can be hard for our hearts to choose.

Paul longed to magnify Christ, whether by life or by death (Philippians 1:21)—but when we are sitting by the bed of our cancer-stricken child, watching her struggle for one more breath and maybe one more day, emotion seems to deliver a knock-out punch to our faith. Job resolved to praise the Lord, even through deep loss. However, when we've said goodbye to our job, our home, our savings, and all earthly hope of security in retirement, it doesn't feel very "glorious." Paul may have been able to glory in his weaknesses when his thorn in the flesh became a permanent part of the décor of his life—but when MS saps your ability to function and restricts you to a wheelchair for decades, your feelings of helplessness and hopelessness can cloud your vision of God's glory.

Following Jesus to Glory

I think of the illustration found in John 21:12–17. The resurrected Jesus had appeared to His disciples on the shores of the Sea of Galilee. Jesus interrogated Peter about his love for the Savior, with the thrice-repeated command "Feed my sheep."

Then He makes this fascinating statement: "Most assuredly, I say to you, when you were younger, you girded yourself and walked where you wished; but when you are old, you will stretch out your hands, and another will gird you and carry you where you do not wish" (v. 18). The writer John comments, "This He spoke, signifying by what death he would glorify God" (v. 19).

Think about this exchange. Jesus describes a very undesirable death as part of Peter's destiny as an obedient disciple. If we could rate our old age or death scenarios, what Jesus described here is "dreadful." Yet John says it is a death that will glorify God.

As many of us would have done, Peter apparently struggled with this revelation. He wanted to know why John (standing nearby) was not going to have the same fate. Jesus offered the frank command to Peter, the second time in this conversation: "Follow Me." Of course, Jesus had just endured the worst possible death, so His example and authority in laying down this command was unquestioned. Jesus also knew the power of resurrection—which Peter also was promised, on the other side of his death.

In fact, Peter would later write these encouraging words, while still anticipating his own difficult final years and eventual death (which according to tradition was an upside-down crucifixion): "But may the God of all grace, who called us to His eternal glory by Christ Jesus, after you have suffered a while, perfect, establish, strengthen, and settle you. To Him be the glory and the dominion forever and ever. Amen" (1 Peter 5:10–11). Peter's deep assurance in the Lord's promise to get us through our "bad" times is remarkable. More remarkable is his strong reminder that we are called to His glory and that it all will culminate in His glory.

Winning the Struggle

So let's just settle it. Praying for God's glory is a struggle. But it is the struggle that can and must be won every day. Our transformation and triumph depend on it.

The Struggle Is Real—and Daily

In my first book, which rose from my own longing to find a biblical and integrated process for daily renewal, I addressed the key issues of my theology, identity, mission, values, priorities, goals, and time. As good as this process was for me, I still drew this conclusion: The hardest thing about the Christian life is that it is so DAILY.[4] Paul reminds us that the outer man is perishing but the inner man is being renewed day by day (2 Corinthians 4:16). There is a sense that every day we live with one hand on the perishables

> *The hardest thing about the Christian life is that it is so DAILY.*

of this life: family, health, job, home, hobbies, plans, etc. In the other hand, we grasp the unseen and eternal reality of thinking, feeling, speaking, acting, and praying, all for God's glory. Our heart has to choose every day to let go of one to grasp fully the other, with both hands—the entirety of our will and personality.

We Are Not Alone in the Struggle

There are people all around us and across the world encountering similar struggles. Perhaps this lends a degree of comfort. But an honest look at the champions of God's glory in the Bible tells us that they are with us in the struggle. Paul "despaired even of life," but came to a place of not trusting in himself but in God (2 Corinthians 1:8). He pled three separate times for the removal of his thorn in the flesh, but eventually came to rest in the grace that could bring strength out of his weakness (2 Corinthians 12:8–10).

Early in his journey of loss, pain, and interpersonal attack, Job said the right words and struggled to do the right thing. In the end, he realized that he needed a deeper revelation of God in order to comprehend His glory (Job 42:1–6).

Perhaps there is no greater comfort than knowing that the Lord Jesus is our High Priest who can "sympathize with our weaknesses" because He "was in all points tempted as we are, yet without sin" (Hebrews 4:15). Included in these temptations is the account of Luke 22:42–44, where He agonized in the garden with the longing of His humanity but the destiny of His deity: "Father, if it is Your will, take this cup away from Me; nevertheless not My will, but Yours, be done." Even this was not easy. "Then an angel appeared to Him from heaven, strengthening Him. And being in agony, He prayed more earnestly. Then His sweat became like great drops of blood falling down to the ground." Jesus understands our struggle. He will strengthen us, even in the depths of distress, to pray earnestly and to grow in our passion that "God would be magnified."

> *Jesus understands our struggle. He will strengthen us, even in the depths of distress, to pray earnestly and to grow in our passion that "God would be magnified."*

Grace to "Go for the Glory"

I define *grace* as God doing for us, in us, and through us what only He can do through the person, power, and presence of Jesus Christ. I have learned that God has tailor-made grace for everything we face. I need the grace to long and pray for His glory. The biblical writer compels us: "Let us therefore come boldly to the throne of grace, that we may obtain mercy and find grace to help in time of need" (Hebrew 4:16).

To Beauty From Ashes

We are encouraged to know that our Lord specializes in taking our broken lives and reluctant hearts and transforming them with a passion for His glory. Bob Rawleigh is a trophy of this truth. Today God is using him as a worship leader and powerful soloist—but it wasn't always this way.

On Bob's ministry Web site, he testifies, "When I was twelve years old, my family went through a series of tragedies that had me reeling until I was in my mid-twenties. By the age of fifteen, my eleven-year-old sister became critically ill, my mother entered the last stages of irreversible schizophrenia, my father came out as a homosexual, and my little brother was running the streets with gangs."[5] Bob's reality changed when he came to Christ in his twenties.

Yet the baggage of his childhood continued to plague Bob's walk with the Lord, his marriage, and his ministry. As he puts it, "The destructive lifestyle of my father brought much evil into my life . . . and the thorns still prick, even to this day." When I met Bob in my office one afternoon, he was broken and looking for the wholeness only Christ can offer.

Through the power of God's truth, an environment of godly acceptance, and regular experiences of worship-based prayer, God restored Bob's spiritual vitality and transformed his heart into a channel of great impact for Christ. He describes it as a journey "to beauty from ashes."

In a recent note from Bob, he wrote, "My life is often like a computer filled with good and bad information. That bad info can create a virus and make the computer malfunction. It then needs to be shut down and rebooted to the mainframe. Worship-based prayer is that rebooting process, and our Father in heaven is the mainframe. Worship-based prayer gives me a priceless opportunity to come into His presence—to be still, and know that He is God. He rids me of bad info, realigns me, and reestablishes me with His will, His kingdom purposes, with His kingdom power. It's all by His Spirit. Because of my human frailty I need rebooting often. Worship-based prayer keeps eternity in my spiritual sight, reminding me not to be overwhelmed by the cares of this temporal life! My love for the Lord gets reignited, and with deep gratitude I want to live to bring Him great glory!"

Let God be magnified.

A Light Bulb Has Been Turned On:
A Trophy of Transformation

Ann Wong is an OB/GYN in the San Francisco Bay area. Having grown up in a Christian home, she believed prayer was both important and necessary as a means by which she talked to God about her needs. She notes, "Extended times of prayer were rare and difficult. In my Christian experience, worship and prayer were in two very different categories."

In 2000, those categories merged as she participated in a women's event that featured multiple days of extended worship-based prayer. "Gazing at His face and worshiping Him for three days straight gave me perspective on all my problems until they seemed so small in comparison to His greatness. I felt that I had experienced a glimpse of heaven and returned home completely transformed with a strong desire to see this level of prayer in my own church."

Like many professionals, Ann leads a very busy life, with additional energy invested in the home and in church leadership. She shares, "Focusing on the face of God rather than on my needs, opened up a new level of intimacy with the Lord and caused me to trust and believe God for things yet to come. It sparked a whole new area of ministry for me. I returned to my church in Sacramento and started a women's prayer ministry. I began prayer-walking at my office, interceding for colleagues, staff, and patients."

The passion to influence others continued to grow. "God put unrest in my heart to move back to my former church in San Jose," Ann says. "Although I did not understand why God was leading me away, I went. Once there, I introduced my pastor and others to worship-based prayer and started a pastor's prayer shield. I also experienced the joy and privilege of leading regular women's prayer, extended times of prayer for our church leadership, prayer retreats for our church, and small-group prayer at prayer summits. God gave our pastor and his wife a vision for our church to become a prayer-saturated church. The vision spreads as God brings a huge awareness and love of prayer to our church. Worship-based prayer was also caught by my sister, Jane, and my brother, Ben, whose desire is to bring a focus of prayer to their respective congregations in northern California and Texas. It is a real joy to hear from others after experiencing worship-based prayer. They say 'a light bulb has been turned on' and express how they love to pray now that they see God in an entirely different way."

CHAPTER 9

How Abiding Guides Our Asking

Just as God's Word must reform our theology,
our ethics, and our practices,
so also must it reform our praying.

D. A. CARSON

If you abide in My word,
you are My disciples indeed.
And you shall know the truth,
and the truth shall make you free.

JESUS—JOHN 8:31–32

Mark Vroegop pastors the rapidly growing College Park Church in Indianapolis, Indiana. Crediting the gracious hand of God, Vroegop believes the profound blessings his church is currently experiencing are the direct result of worship-based prayer.

Mark's own journey of spiritual renewal was reignited at a retreat with pastors from his area. At first, Mark and his wife, Sarah, were reluctant to attend. For most of their ministry life, their church activities had been restricted to the Baptist circles where they found common theological agreement. This retreat would include a broad representation of denominations, creating possible moments of discomfort or conflict.

More significantly, Mark and Sarah were feeling fragile.

After having three healthy sons, their first daughter, Sylvia, was stillborn. They were pregnant again and feeling anxious and guarded about the baby. In spite of these reservations, they spent three days worshiping the Lord from His Word in the company of other pastors and spouses from the region. In separate experiences, they both found the Scripture and the Spirit drawing them to open their hearts to their ministry peers. In one room during an afternoon session, Sarah was surrounded with tearful, praying women crying out to God for healing of her broken heart and the Lord's hand of grace on the new life in her womb. Next door, Mark wept before his ministry peers about his own internal fears, concerns for his wife, and anxieties about the pregnancy. With profound compassion, pastors from many denominations placed their hands on Mark, entreating the Lord for restored trust and confidence.

Mark describes it as a profound, life-changing experience. The power of praying from the Scriptures in the company of other believers brought healing and hope to their hearts—as spouses and parents. Mark discovered an incredible unity with leaders from other churches in the Lord's presence. After this experience, Mark began to pray and lead in a brand-new way. (And, he and Sarah soon became the parents of a beautiful, healthy little girl named Savannah.)

Prior to this weekend, Mark says his prayer life was "mostly focused on request-based praying." His attempts to pray with others were often "dry and boring." He notes, "I knew that praying with others was important, but it was a real chore!" This dynamic young pastor explains, "More than anything, worship-based prayer has made me a more passionate lover of Jesus. I see His Word and prayer as means, not ends. Worship-based prayer has helped me to see that the ultimate aim of my time with the Lord or with others before the Lord is worship. It is the starting point and the goal."

God's Voice—Our Ear

It is so easy in our perfunctory approach to prayer to blow into God's presence, conduct our daily data dump to be relieved of our worries but not revived in our worship. Calvin Miller explains, "Too often, we go into God's presence with a list of pleas, trying to talk God into granting our desire. But this kind of praying makes us 'one big mouth' and God 'one grand ear.' But when we pray the Scriptures, it makes God the voice and leaves us as the ear. In short, God gets His turn at getting a word in edgewise."[1]

One core focus of worship-based prayer is the commitment to always start our prayers from the Word of God. This is the key to abiding. Jesus emphasized, "If you abide in Me, and My Words abide in you, you will ask what you desire, and it shall be done for you. By this My Father is glorified, that you bear much fruit; so you will be My disciples" (John 15:7–8).

> *One core focus of worship-based prayer is the commitment to always start our prayers from the Word of God. This is the key to abiding.*

In John 15, Jesus gave His disciples the powerful metaphor of fruitfulness in their spiritual lives. Just as a branch abides in the vine, deriving its life and productivity from the provision of the vine, so we find our life and source in Him. One result of this abiding is powerful guidance and confidence in prayer.

Abiding and Abundance

What does it mean to *abide*? The word means to "continue, remain, dwell, or stay." It is the idea of a life-giving connection with Christ that produces His character and accomplishes His will in us. As Charles Spurgeon noted, *abiding* means "yielding ourselves up to Him to receive His life and to let that life work out its results in us. We live *in* Him, *by* Him, *for* Him, *to* Him when we abide in Him."[2] My friend Bud McCord speaks of abiding in this way: "Jesus in us is the perfection we need to live the Christian life on a moment by moment basis."[3] Jesus in us is the perfection we must have to pray.

If prayer is to be more than lists and the language of human reason, we must grasp this command, making the worship-focused relationship with Christ our first desire. Then His Word in us can shape all that we are—and all that we think, especially in prayer. When this happens, our prayers are transformed and so are we.

Clearly, this is the idea of a truth-based intimacy that shapes our prayers and forms the proper expression of our needs. Again, prayer is not a casual recitation of whatever pains and problems pop into our minds on any given occasion. It is the overflow of a heart focused on the conscious presence of Christ, clinging to Him and His Word as the source and scope of our lives.

Pastor John Piper gives the right perspective when he says:

> There are dozens of instances in the Bible of people praying for desires as natural as the desire for protection from enemies and escape from danger and success in vocation and fertility in marriage, recovery from sickness, etc. My point is not that those desires are wrong. My point is that they should always be subordinate to spiritual desires; kingdom desires; fruit-bearing desires; gospel-spreading, God-centered desires; Christ-exalting, God-glorifying desires. And when our natural desires are felt as a means to these greater desires, then they become the proper subject of prayer.[4]

What is the result of this Scripture-fueled abiding that leads us to ask with bold assurance? It is the glory of the Father—through a life that bears much fruit. Already in this discourse, Jesus has spoken of bearing fruit—and more fruit. Now He describes much fruit. If we abide in Him, we bear fruit. If He prunes us, we bear more fruit. If we abide in Him, with His truth controlling our hearts, we bear much fruit. A. W. Pink described this fruit as "Christlike affections, dispositions, grace, as well as the works in which they are displayed,"[5] adding that *fruit* is "the outflow of our union with Christ; only thus will it be traced to its true origin and source."

Praying With an Open Bible

While it was not always this way, all of my praying in the last two decades, both personal and in community, has begun with an open Bible. On a personal level, I read the Scriptures using the Bible program on my laptop. As specific passages speak to me, I paste them into my journal program. Then I take time to allow those Bible segments to speak deeply to my heart and write out my prayers in response. This sense of Christ's presence and the substance of His Word guide my praying for that day. When I miss a day of this kind of praying, which is more often than I wish, I feel the difference and the distance.

George Muller, the renowned man of faith and evangelist who cared for thousands of orphans and established dozens of Christian schools in the 1800s, spoke about the vital role of Scripture in his prayer life. He noted that for years he tried to pray without starting in the Bible in the morning. Inevitably, his mind wandered sometimes for ten, fifteen, even thirty minutes.[6] Then, when he began to start each morning with the Bible to nourish his soul, he found his heart being transformed by the truth, resulting in spontaneous prayers of confession, thanksgiving, intercession, and supplication. This became his daily experience for decades, resulting in great personal growth and power for life and ministry.

In his autobiography, Muller noted that this kind of prayer is . . .

> . . . *not the simple reading of the Word of God, so that it only passes through our minds, just as water runs through a pipe, but considering what we read, pondering over it, and applying it to our hearts. When we pray, we speak to God. Now, prayer, in order to be continued for any length of time in any other than a formal manner, requires, generally speaking, a measure of strength or godly desire, and the season, therefore, when this exercise of the soul can be most effectually performed is after the inner man has been nourished by meditation on the Word of God, where we find our Father speaking to us,*

to encourage us, to comfort us, to instruct us, to humble us, to reprove us.[7]

On-Target Prayers

Speaking about this very idea, John Piper says, "I have seen that those whose prayers are most saturated with Scripture are generally most fervent and most effective in prayer. And where the mind isn't brimming with the Bible, the heart is not generally brimming with prayer."[8] When we do not begin our prayers from this posture of abiding, allowing the Word to saturate our minds and guide our words, our prayers can become short, superficial, shallow, and even selfish.

"Where the mind isn't brimming with the Bible, the heart is not generally brimming with prayer."

Every year I sign up to volunteer for the state's Department of Natural Resources, assisting them in the population control of certain animals that regularly endanger drivers by darting in front of oncoming cars. This is also known as deer hunting. Every hunter's harvest is only as good as his aim. One way to guarantee an empty-handed hunt is to inadvertently knock the scope on your rifle out of proper alignment. Usually hunters take great care in assuring that the scope is accurate by visiting a shooting range before going to gather food for the winter. If your gun is off at the scope, it will be off at the target.

When our prayers are off at the source, they will fall short in our satisfaction and kingdom success. Prayers, like a bullet from a gun, get more off-target the further they go. When we get into a routine of simply praying our own ideas and thoughts, our prayers are increasingly misguided. The longer we do this, the further we travel from God's design for prayer. I have noticed that people who have prayed from religious formality or even traditional list-based recitations are often entrenched in their approach and resistant to coming back to a fresh understanding of the power of Scripture-fed, Spirit-led prayers. Pastors speak with me often about the unreasonable resistance they face when trying to move people in their church from a request-based paradigm to a worship-based approach.

Praying on the Same Page

A worship-based focus on the face of Christ and His Word is a powerful approach to group prayer, as well. Since 1994, I have known the deep joy of leading a variety of prayer retreats every year. These multi-day gatherings have no agenda, speakers, or special music. Those who have never participated in an experience like this wonder what we do to fill the time. In reality, these retreats could be labeled "Word summits" because the vast majority of our praying springs from massive doses of spontaneous Scripture reading offered by any participant who feels led to read aloud. Because God's Word is such a limitless treasure of truth, with countless applications to the human heart, we never run out of material.

Inevitably, the Holy Spirit weaves these passages together in a cohesive way to direct us into specific themes of prayer. Very often, one single passage grips the heart of an individual and becomes the basis of personal meditation and an eventual life-changing response.

I have experienced the power of Word-based praying in many other contexts as well. For many years I have gathered with church members early on Sunday mornings for prayer, in anticipation of and preparation for the Sunday services. We simply progress through the Psalms, reading one together, and then allowing the Scripture, under the Spirit's leadership, to guide us in our prayers. (I will explain this approach in more detail in part 3.) Currently, I am in my fifth tour through the Psalms in the context of this Sunday morning prayer time. One of the participants, a pastor in his sixties, often says, "I have never prayed like this before. Often I plan to sleep in but usually can't because I am so excited about discovering how the Psalms are going to delight our hearts and show us how to pray."

For fifteen years I gathered at six o'clock on Monday mornings to pray with the men of my church. As early as it was (and as hard as it was for me to be up and out the door so early on a

Monday, after a very busy Sunday), God always delighted our hearts as we started not with lists of needs but with His Word.

Who Starts the Prayer Conversation?

In a sense, prayer is a continual conversation between our hearts and God's. Nevertheless, when we stop to spend time in focused prayer, it is important to know who should start the conversation. If prayer is simply the discharge of my own will and thoughts, in the hope that I can help God run the universe, then I should start the prayer conversation. On the other hand, if prayer is about my heart becoming intimate and aligned with the heart of the Savior, then I should let Him start the conversation. This is the reality of abiding in Him and letting His words abide in us.

I have experienced this joy so many times. Some mornings, when I do not even know my own heart, let alone what I should pray about, God's Word brings light and clarity. The truth exposes issues in my heart that, left to my own reason, I would have never recognized. Referring to the truth of Christ's words abiding in us (John 15:7), author A. W. Pink writes, "Note it is not here 'my Word' but 'my words.' It is not the Word as a whole, but the Word, as it were, broken up. It is the precepts and promises of Scripture personally appropriated, fed upon by faith, hidden in the heart . . . until its contents become the substance of our innermost being."[9]

> The best way to talk to God is from a heart passionate for Christ and with language springing from His Word.

This then, is a crucial component for transforming prayer and a key to our worship-based approach. Indeed the best way to talk to God is from a heart passionate for Christ and with language springing from His Word. Then we have the confidence of praying His heart and His will. Andrew Murray reminds us, "The entrance His words find in me will be the measure of the power of my words with Him. What God's words are to me, is the test of what He Himself is to me, and so of the uprightness of my desire after Him in prayer."[10] Murray also notes, "In His words His will is revealed. As the words abide in me, His will rules me; my will becomes the empty vessel which His will fills, the willing instrument which His will wields; He fills my inner being."[11]

Imagine what a difference it would make if we went straight to the Word of God to hear from Him and then based our prayer time in His wisdom, not ours. Consider what insight and direction we would receive if we asked, in the context of prayer, "Lord, what is on your heart? What truth does the Holy Spirit want us to pray about?" Yes, many of the same needs would surface, but from a different perspective—God's, not ours. The way we pray about our needs would change. With the faith that comes from the Word of God, and the passion that comes from the indwelling Christ, we would pray differently.

A Breath of Life and Prayer

Pastor Mark Vroegop, reflecting again on the change in his prayer life, shares: "Previously, I didn't really understand the full potential of what adoration and worship could really be like. I had no understanding about the role of the Scriptures in informing what I pray about or how I prayed. My Bible reading and my prayer times were completely separated and not connected."

Today, prayer is transforming Mark's leadership and his congregation, with dynamic impact on the community. He writes, "It was amazing to me how much life and energy was breathed into our prayer meeting by simply changing the focus to seeking God's face, not just His hand. It resonated with my heart and there seemed to be no end as to what we could say to God about himself from His Word. Further, when we started with the right focus, it led to wonderful seasons of confession and powerful moments of intercession. There was a real sense that we were not in control, and that God was speaking to us through His Word. I have often said that a worship-based prayer experience where Word, song, and prayer are spontaneously offered feels like it must be close to what was happening in the early church. It just seems so right!"

Speaking in specific terms about the impact of this Scripture-fed approach, Vroegop testifies, "Worship-based prayer has increased my passion for Jesus. Worshiping Him through prayer has often helped me through very difficult seasons, broken me over my sin, provided strength when I was ready to give up, and emboldened my faith. I have seen God do things in a prayer meeting that have been startling. I know people who were changed through the prayers of others. I know people who came under conviction and received Christ while in a prayer meeting. I know people who had their needs met within hours of praying with others. Before worship-based prayer, I *believed* that prayer worked; now I *know* it does."

Perhaps this is the very reality Andrew Murray embraced when he wrote, "It is the Word of Christ, loved, lived in, abiding in us, becoming through obedience and action part of our being, that makes us one with Christ, that fits us spiritually for touching, for taking hold of God."[12] John Stott summarizes it well: "It is only when Christ's words abide in us that our prayers will be answered. Then we can ask what we will and it shall be done, because we shall will only what He wills."[13]

CHAPTER 10

How His Spirit Ignites Our Supplication

Every manifestation of the power of the flesh in us
and weakness of our spiritual life
must drive us to the conviction that God will,
through the powerful operation of His Holy Spirit,
work out a new and strong life in us. . . .
Yes, let us believe that the Spirit
who is in us is the Spirit of the Lord Jesus,
and that He is in us to make us truly partakers of His life.
If we firmly believe this and set our hearts upon it,
then there will come a change in our intercourse with the Word and prayer
such as we could not have thought possible.
Believe it firmly; expect it surely.

ANDREW MURRAY

When He, the Spirit of truth, has come,
He will guide you into all truth;
for He will not speak on His own authority,
but whatever He hears He will speak;
and He will tell you things to come.
He will glorify Me, for He will take of what is Mine
and declare it to you.

JESUS—JOHN 16:13–14

If you had unlimited resources and wanted your children to
become extremely proficient in their learning, you would hire

a tutor. You would have the freedom to spare no expense and to acquire a knowledgeable, highly skilled teacher who would come to your home and personally assure your children the best education possible.

Our Father, with His unlimited resources, and His commitment to teach us to pray, has given us a supernatural tutor. The Holy Spirit is available to us and resides within us 24/7. Our Father longs for intimacy with us and knows that real prayer is impossible apart from the indwelling Spirit. We are enabled to "worship God in the Spirit, rejoice in Christ Jesus, and have no confidence in the flesh" (Philippians 3:3) through worship-based prayer. The Holy Spirit empowers us to know Christ. Worship-based prayer brings us to a greater sensitivity and surrender to the Holy Spirit. As a result, our prayers become Spirit-fueled. And we are transformed.

> *Worship-based prayer brings us to a greater sensitivity and surrender to the Holy Spirit. As a result, our prayers become Spirit-fueled. And we are transformed.*

Almost Dead but Fully Alive

Recently my wife and I spoke at a women's gathering on a Saturday morning. After the breakfast, a mother and daughter from our church gave the first presentation. We were slated to follow them on the program. Their story was riveting.

Linda Barrick and her daughter, Jen, gave an account of the events that took place on a Sunday evening, November 5, 2006. As the family drove home from church, a drunk driver traveling eighty miles per hour struck their minivan head-on. The father, Andy, and Linda were in the front. Fifteen-year-old Jen and eleven-year-old Josh were in the back. All sustained life-threatening injuries. They were rushed to emergency rooms at different hospitals.

While all four family members were in serious condition, doctors did not expect Jen to live through the night. But God sustained her life. She remained in a coma for five weeks with traumatic brain injuries and multiple skull fractures. Jen's slow emergence from the coma took many more weeks. Doctors feared the brain injuries might prompt a flurry of strange behaviors such as screaming or cursing. Instead, Jen's spirit poured out with praise songs and constant prayers. Even though she was not cognizant of her injuries, her location, or even the names of her family members, she continued to praise God. Her mom commented, "The Holy Spirit was so alive and evident in her."

Unable to open her eyes or comprehend her surroundings, Linda says her daughter literally prayed for hours. "But she did not ask for one thing," recounts Linda. "Even with her body thrashing back and forth uncontrollably, she would cry out for hours, 'Lord, you are so good. Lord, you are so faithful.'" Linda notes, "I would just sit there and weep as the Spirit enabled her to praise her Father, sing worship songs, and even quote Scriptures. It was as if she had been in His presence the whole time."[1]

Today, Jen is still in the recovery process, suffers memory loss, and endures cortical blindness. Yet she is able and eager to join her mother regularly in telling the amazing account of God's grace and the power of prayer.

As Rosemary and I listened to the Barricks' story, I was struck by this example of the Holy Spirit's intention to produce truth-based worship and thanksgiving in the hearts of His children. Beyond our mental and physical capacities exists a spiritual dimension that we must grasp if we are going to learn to pray by the power of the Holy Spirit.

Worship-based prayer brings our hearts into intimate harmony with the person of the Holy Spirit and enhances our surrender to His control, wisdom, and power for our prayers. The Spirit then enables us to worship more fully. This worship, in turn, brings us into a deeper reality of the Spirit's life, thus continuing the circle.

Jen Barrick, with limited mental and physical capacity, exhibited a profound experience of prayer in the realm of the Holy Spirit. Many of us depend on our own intellect and forget the Holy Spirit's essential role. We may punch the prayer clock, but transformation eludes us.

Graveyard or Insane Asylum

My friend Jim Cymbala urges Christians toward a vibrant and practical reliance on the Holy Spirit. He strongly notes that when it comes to the person of the Holy Spirit, churches tend to be either cemeteries or insane asylums. Some hardly recognize the Holy Spirit or seek Him at all. Others engage in all kinds of bizarre, extra-biblical antics, for which the Holy Spirit gets "credit." In our prayers, we want to avoid these extremes, but must set our hearts on the very real, powerful, and practical reality of the Holy Spirit.

In his book *Forgotten God*, Francis Chan writes, "From my perspective, the Holy Spirit is tragically neglected and, for all practical purposes, forgotten. While no evangelical would deny His existence, I'm willing to bet there are millions of church-goers across America who cannot confidently say they have experienced His presence or action in their lives over the past year. And many of them do not believe they can."[2] He continues, "If I were Satan and my ultimate goal was to thwart God's kingdom and purposes, one of my main strategies would be to get churchgoers to ignore the Holy Spirit . . . but when believers live in the power of the Spirit, the evidence in their lives is supernatural. The church cannot help but be different, and the world cannot help but notice."[3]

> *"If I were Satan and my ultimate goal was to thwart God's kingdom and purposes, one of my main strategies would be to get churchgoers to ignore the Holy Spirit."*

Not only does Jesus want His house (people) to be characterized by prayer (Mark 11:17), He wants us to be controlled and empowered by the supernatural reality of His Holy Spirit rather than by human strategies and intellectual prowess.

Word, Spirit, and Worship

We've seen that prayer is best experienced with an open Bible. We read the biblical text, looking for great truths about

God. These truths fuel our worship as we engage in prayer and song, in reverence for His name, character, and works. Our meditation and application of these truths becomes powerful as we open our hearts to the Spirit. These are the essentials of transformation.

Paul describes this dynamic in Colossians 3:16. Even though the context of this experience is in community, the same truth applies individually. He writes, "Let the word of Christ dwell in you richly in all wisdom, teaching and admonishing one another in psalms and hymns and spiritual songs, singing with grace in your hearts to the Lord." God's Word is a stimulus to worship and a tool for worship.

Compare that passage with Ephesians 5:18–20, where it says, "And do not be drunk with wine, in which is dissipation; but be filled with the Spirit, speaking to one another in psalms and hymns and spiritual songs, singing and making melody in your heart to the Lord, giving thanks always for all things to God the Father in the name of our Lord Jesus Christ."

The parallels between Word and Spirit are obvious. When we are under the control of the Holy Spirit, worship overflows. When we are engaged with the Scriptures, worship abounds.

The "Game Changers" of Prayer

Now read carefully these words:

> *But as it is written: "Eye has not seen, nor ear heard, nor have entered into the heart of man the things which God has prepared for those who love Him." But God has revealed them to us through His Spirit. For the Spirit searches all things, yes, the deep things of God. For what man knows the things of a man except the spirit of the man which is in him? Even so no one knows the things of God except the Spirit of God. Now we have received, not the spirit of the world, but the Spirit who is from God, that we might know the things that have been freely given to us by God. (1 Corinthians 2:9–12)*

Read it again. In my heart, this passage has such a wow factor when it comes to prayer. I ask myself, "Do I just want a perfunctory experience of human reason and religious ritual in my prayer times? Or do I want something supernatural to occur as I come to understand the deep things of God? Do I just want to go through the routines of prayer requests and duplicated sheets of lists created by what others think I should pray about? Or do I want to receive the things the Spirit wants to freely give to me as I pray from God's Word in surrender and sensitivity to His leadership?" Our answers to these questions are game changers in our prayer life—and life changers in our spiritual journey.

Concerning this idea, John Calvin wrote, "The testimony of the Spirit is superior to reason. For as God alone can properly bear witness to his own words, so these words will not obtain full credit in the hearts of men, until they are sealed by the inward testimony of the Spirit."[4]

Puritan William Law added great application for us: "Read whatever chapter of Scripture you will, and be ever so delighted with it—yet it will leave you as poor, as empty and unchanged as it found you unless it has turned you wholly and solely to the Spirit of God, and brought you into full union with and dependence upon Him."[5]

Those who have adopted a worship-based approach of seeking God's face first and foremost *have* experienced this amazing reality. God's Spirit takes God's Word and ignites our heart with truth, wisdom, direction, focus, and passion in our prayer experiences. Once you have tasted this kind of prayer, you never want to go back. This is why God longs for us to pray in the Spirit.

Praying in the Spirit

What exactly is "praying in the Spirit" and what does it accomplish? Let's start with a definition. Some have reduced "praying in the Spirit" to a certain expression of emotion or the crafting of special language in order to solicit God's blessings. In truth, it is much clearer and deeper than any of these modern notions. Greek scholar Kenneth Wuest noted: "Praying in the Spirit is praying in dependence on the Holy Spirit. It is prayer exercised in the sphere of the Holy Spirit, motivated and empowered by Him."[6] Pastor John Piper defines it simply: "Praying in the Holy Spirit is to be moved and guided by the Holy Spirit in prayer. We pray by His power and according to His direction."[7]

Thomas Goodwin, another great Puritan, said, "The Holy Spirit, who is the Intercessor within us, and who searches the deep things of God, doth offer, prompt and suggest to us in our prayers those very things that are in God's heart, to grant the thing we desire of Him so as it often comes to pass that a poor creature is carried on to speak God's very heart to Himself, and then God cannot, nor doth not deny."[8] Praying in the Spirit is vital to worship—to knowing God's heart. Then we can pray His agenda with confidence as requests are actually prompted by the Spirit, not the flesh.

Clear Communication

In my seven years of undergraduate and graduate studies, I got pretty decent grades—except for one class. I definitely did not excel in Probability and Statistics. This was partly due to the difficulty of the subject for a non-math-oriented guy. However, a big part of the problem was the lack of comprehensible communication from the professor. He had recently immigrated to the United States. He was highly intelligent, and I think he understood and spoke English pretty proficiently. However, his accent was so thick that I could not understand what he was saying. I even met with him in his office several times, seeking further explanation on the classwork. In time, we both became frustrated by my inability to grasp what he was saying. I basically gave up and settled for the first and last D of my college and seminary studies.

In the school of prayer and Christian living, the subject is not simply difficult—it is supernatural. Fortunately, we have a supernatural teacher in the Holy Spirit. The good news is that He speaks clearly, specifically, and helpfully, so that we can understand exactly what we need to know.

Spirit Scriptures

Eastern religions, and even some teachers of the Christian faith, propose that the best way to hear from God's Spirit (or maybe some other spirit) is to empty your mind, accompanied by various breathing exercises. That might be a great way to get a *D* in Prayer. Rather, the Scriptures affirm the best way to hear from the Spirit is to fill the mind with the Word of God, accompanied by careful reading and meditation on the sacred text. That's the best way to receive what the Spirit is speaking clearly.

Let's look at a few more verses that help us grasp and anticipate His work in communicating the truths of prayer proficiency to our hearts. Ephesians 6:10–20 is the culmination of Paul's teaching on spiritual warfare and the armor of God so vital to our victory. In verse 17, he speaks of the "sword of the Spirit, which is the word of God." With God's Word deep in our hearts and ready on our lips, we are told to be "praying always with all prayer and supplication *in the Spirit*, being watchful to this end with all perseverance and supplication for all the saints" (v. 18). We learn here that praying in the Spirit fuels passion, consistency, an alert mind, endurance, and insight in how to pray for the many people God puts on our hearts.

Consider Jude 20–21, where it says, "But you, beloved, building yourselves up on your most holy faith, *praying in the Holy Spirit*, keep yourselves in the love of God, looking for the mercy of our Lord Jesus Christ unto eternal life." Jude had been describing those who do not have the Spirit, embrace false teaching, and unleash a destructive impact on the church (Jude 19). In contrast, he says we can grow in strength and stability as we pray in the realm of the Spirit. We pray in direct connection to our most holy faith, which is the revealed truth of the Scriptures (see Jude 3-4). The result is that we "keep ourselves" fully engaged in the assurance and experience of the love of God. God is our keeper and preserver (as we see in Jude 1 and 24), but prayer in the Spirit is the means of keeping our love relationship with Him vibrant. Praying in the Spirit also cultivates hopeful expectation of the return of Christ.

Look at Romans 8:26–30:

> *Likewise the Spirit also helps in our weaknesses. For we do not know what we should pray for as we ought, but the Spirit Himself makes intercession for us with groanings which cannot be uttered. Now He who searches the hearts knows what the mind of the Spirit is, because He makes intercession for the saints according to the will of God. And we know that all things work together for good to those who love God, to those who are the called according to His purpose. For whom He foreknew, He also predestined to be conformed to the image of His Son, that He might be the firstborn among many brethren. Moreover whom He predestined, these He also called; whom He called, these He also justified; and whom He justified, these He also glorified.*

Even the apostle Paul confesses that in our mere human intellect, we are not able to pray effectively. Our minds and hearts are weak. The Holy Spirit moves and prays within us, in perfect harmony with the will of the Father and the Son. The Spirit works in us to tutor us in prayer according to the will of God, as we have assurance of God's goodness and sovereignty in the unfolding of the events of our lives (Romans 8:28). The Spirit works in us to make us like Jesus (v. 29) and to keep transforming us until we are in glory with Him (v. 30). J. Oswald Sanders wrote, "Prayer in the Spirit is prayer whose supreme object is the glory of God, and only in a secondary sense is it a blessing for ourselves or for others."[9]

Our minds and hearts are weak. The Holy Spirit moves and prays within us, in perfect harmony with the will of the Father and the Son. The Spirit works in us to tutor us in prayer according to the will of God.

We experience transforming prayer. This, I believe, is what Jen Barrick experienced during her slow recovery in a hospital bed. And it is what God desires for us in our prayer lives.

His Goal—Our Choice

I fly a lot these days, traveling to conferences and churches. As you know, at the beginning of every flight an attendant (or in some cases a video) gives clear, life-saving instructions to passengers on how to stay safe and what to do in the case of an emergency. I am often listening to music on my iPod rather than paying attention to the very familiar drill. Sometimes an attendant will come by and tell me to turn off my music and listen. I understand she is not trying to be mean; she is simply trying to help me receive the vital information I need to fly safely.

Of course, the reason many of us tune out the pre-flight orientation is that we have heard it so many times before. This familiarity can lead to ignorance and perhaps tragedy. The flight attendants are there to prevent this.

Prayer is a very familiar idea to many of us. We are also accustomed to the truth of the Holy Spirit in our lives. Like the road-warrior frequent flyer, we may tune out the instructions we need because we are so familiar with the experience. However, unlike a flight, where the instructions and routines are usually predictable, there should be nothing mundane or standard about our prayer times. Every conversation with God—every encounter with His presence—is as fresh and essential as our next breath. We cannot tune out the instruction of the Word and the Spirit. This guidance is a lifesaver in our walk with Christ and the key to getting an *A* in Prayer.

Jesus prepared us for this profound experience. In John 16:13–14 He says, "However, when He, the Spirit of truth, has come, He will guide you into all truth; for He will not speak on His own authority, but whatever He hears He will speak; and He will tell you things to come. He will glorify Me, for He will take of what is Mine and declare it to you."

Every one of us is confronted with a choice. Will we allow familiarity to breed apathy and ineffectiveness as we tune out the vital instructions? Will we be content to simply pray from our own intellectual framework of understanding, with potentially careless and endless lists of ideas that have not been surrendered to the power of the Word and the Spirit? Will we merely seek God's hand to get what we think we need to get by for another week as we hurry in and out of His presence? Or will we seek His face, from His Word, by His Spirit, as we learn to pray in a life-transforming fashion? Jesus promised clear guidance, insight, and a life that brings Him glory. We must take out our ear buds of tradition and apathy and listen. It will change our lives.

A Soul-Cleansing Experience:
A Trophy of Transformation

Every Christian has faced an assignment from God that feels way above his or her experience or abilities. We can feel over-whelmed, intimidated, and even hopeless. Harry Li, a Chinese-American electrical engineering professor, struggled with these emotions when God called him from his comfortable profession to serve as a pastor at a small, diverse church plant in the heart of Little Rock, Arkansas, where most churches are highly seg-regated. "I felt like a drowning man who was responsible for teaching others how to swim!" he says.

During his second year as pastor, he attended a multi-day prayer retreat for pastors. "I had no expectations but plenty of hesitation about committing three days from my busy sched-ule to prayer. I did not think it would be possible to pray for that length of time." In looking back at that defining moment, he says, "It blew me away! It was mind-boggling! Amazing! Earth-shattering! Worship-based prayer was not boring. It was life-giving, engaging, and exciting! Never before had I expe-rienced prayer that left me feeling so incredibly strengthened, encouraged, and supernaturally empowered.

"That soul-cleansing experience changed me, period. It changed my understanding of God, of prayer, of myself, and my calling into ministry. My walk with God is deeper than before and it has led to a greater understanding of the role of the Holy Spirit in my life, which, in turn, led to more effective ministry."

This Spirit-produced experience of change was so real for Harry that he became a change-agent in his city. He was convinced that the greatest gift he could give to the body of Christ, where many others struggled to embrace God's call and power, was to organize pastors to pray together. Not only did Harry's confidence and impact in his local church soar, but he now organizes multi-day regional pastors' prayer gath-erings in Little Rock. "In this role, I have seen the Lord do some great things among His people," he says. "The body of Christ is being mobilized and unified like never before—in answer to prayer!

"My church would be the first to say they have seen God's hand in my life and that I have grown up in front of them all. The tremendous spiritual growth I've experienced in the last eight years is entirely attributed to understanding prayer. If I had not discovered worship-based prayer, I doubt I would be in ministry today."

CHAPTER 11

How His Name Corrects Our Nonsense

Prayer is a means God uses to give us what he wants.

W. BINGHAM HUNTER

Therefore God also has highly exalted Him
and given Him the name which is above every name.

THE APOSTLE PAUL—PHILIPPIANS 2:9

For high school graduation, my parents gave me the Dale Carnegie Course. This training, which Carnegie started in 1912, inspires confidence for public speaking and provides tools for winning friends and influencing people. At seventeen years old, the course taught me a lot about human nature and helped me get out of my introverted box.

A key principle they taught was the necessity of remembering names. Carnegie believed that a person's name is the most important sound in any language. It is their unique identifier.

However, behind this technique of remembering names is still the desire to win friends and influence people, which is ultimately about personal advancement. Remembering a name is a tool to get people to like you, respond to you, and help you succeed in life. It is not always the expression of a genuine concern for the real needs or interests of the other person.

There is no name like the name of Jesus Christ. Knowing

the power of His name, most of us remember to tack it on to our prayers virtually every time we pray. However, like Carnegie's students, our reason for remembering His name may be for our own purposes, not His.

Truth or Tradition?

Over the years, I have prayed for a lot of pretty crazy things "in Jesus' name." In college, I asked for a date with a particular girl, an improved grade on a final exam, and to win the election for student body president. Many believers invoke Jesus' name in order to get a prime parking spot, a pay raise, or even a winning lottery ticket. Like me, maybe you have used the "in Jesus' name" mantra like some kind of magical charm to coerce God into giving you something you really wanted—or thought you needed.

> *Most of us know the idea of praying in Jesus' name is far beyond the routine of adding these three words on the end of a prayer. Yet when we do not do it, we feel almost heretical. It is the traditional thing to do.*

Most of us know the idea of praying in Jesus' name is far beyond the routine of adding these three words on the end of a prayer. Yet when we do not do it, we feel almost heretical. It is the traditional thing to do. In group or public prayers, it is a given that whoever prays better wrap it up "in Jesus' name." When they fail to do so, they may get a few raised eyebrows and words of doubt about the spiritual legitimacy of their prayers. After all, will God really hear their prayers if they fail to include this three-word add-on?

Turn Your Eyes Upon Jesus

One of the amazing benefits of a worship-based approach to prayer is that it fundamentally takes our eyes off ourselves and fixes them on Christ. We establish our prayer experience on Him, not ourselves. We seek to pray His thoughts, not our own.

As the Spirit takes the conductor's wand of the Scriptures

and orchestrates our praying, we cannot help but turn our eyes upon Jesus and "look full in His wonderful face." Then, as the hymn continues, "the things of earth will grow strangely dim in the light of His glory and grace."[1] At that moment of wonder and intimacy we are really in the place to truly pray in Jesus' name, regardless of the final three words of the prayer.

A popular worship song says, "It's all about you, Jesus," and leads us to acknowledge that our lives are really not about our own agendas. We recognize that Jesus is God and our response is to surrender to His ways. In my years of learning about and leading others in prayer, I have found this to become the heart reality of what the Lord accomplishes as we pray. This is the path to praying in Jesus' name.

What's in a Name?

The first formal mention of prayer in the Bible occurs in Genesis 4:26, "Then men began to call on the name of the Lord." The "name of the Lord" represents more than a title for God. It is the essence of His identity and character revealed to the hearts of men. This passage pictures humanity's first response to God's revelation of himself, crying aloud to Him in prayer. The centerpiece of this praying was the name or the character of God. It would not be a stretch to say that this first expression of prayer was, at heart, a cry of worship.

God reveals himself in His names throughout the Scriptures.[2] If you have been a Christian for a long time, you could probably pause now and think of some of those names from the Old Testament. There is a real sense in which all prayer is ultimately a response to the name of God. One writer says, "As the

There is a real sense in which all prayer is ultimately a response to the name of God.

people of God respond in worship, they 'magnify' the name of the Lord (Psalm 34:3; 69:30): that is, they rejoice in what God's name reveals about his nature, and at the same time they pray that God will be true to himself."[3]

Jesus continued this focus on God's name when He taught His disciples that the first expression of all prayer is "Our Father in heaven, hallowed be Your *name*" (Matthew 6:9). Christ introduced His followers to a new reality of God as their personal and intimate Father, which would become personal and powerful through His saving work. Jesus taught that prayer is a response to the name of God—which is holy, revered, and worthy of our worship.

In the New Testament, we learn that Jesus came to earth "in My Father's *name*" (John 5:43). He spoke often of His mission to do His Father's will for His Father's glory (John 4:34; 5:30; 17:4). He explained His perfect union with the heart and character of the Father (John 5:19; 8:28; 8:42). And He said, "I and the Father are one" (John 10:30 NIV).

My Name Is Jesus, and . . .

Throughout His ministry, Jesus brought great clarity to us about His character and identity by declaring His unique names. The fullness of God in Christ becomes clear. Old Testament truth comes to light, like a slowly rising sun, to the hearts of His disciples. He is "Wonderful, Counselor, Mighty God, Everlasting Father, Prince of Peace. Of the increase of His government and peace there will be no end" (Isaiah 9:6–7).

This is God's gracious work in drawing us to a deeper knowledge of Him and a greater response in prayer. He excited their worship, for example, with the "I am" statements Jesus made in the gospel of John:

- "I am the bread of life" (John 6:35).
- "I am the light of the world" (John 8:12; 9:5).
- "I am the gate for the sheep" (John 10:7, 9 NIV).
- "I am the good shepherd" (John 10:14).
- "I am the resurrection and the life" (John 11:25).
- "I am the way, the truth, and the life" (John 14:6).
- "I am the true vine" (15:1, 5).

Later, the New Testament books will explode additional truths about our Christ, telling us that He is the Alpha and the Omega (Revelation 1:8), the author and finisher of our faith (Hebrews 12:2), the chief cornerstone of the household of God (Ephesians 2:20), the head of the church (Ephesians 1:22), the very Word of God (Revelation 19:13), and the King of Kings and the Lord of Lords (Revelation 19:16). Again, these are more than name tags on the lapel of His robe. These are powerful revelations of His character that empower our worship and prayers.

A New Normal

In Jesus' final upper room gathering with His disciples, He taught, "No one comes to the Father except through Me" (John 14:6) and "He who has seen Me has seen the Father" (John 14:9). Then in the same breath, He opens a window of new understanding about prayer before His followers. Because of Jesus' divinity, union with the Father, miraculous works, and supernatural commission He will give to His disciples, He now establishes a profound new normal in prayer. Read carefully: "Most assuredly, I say to you, he who believes in Me, the works that I do he will do also; and greater works than these he will do, because I go to My Father. And whatever you ask in *My name*, that I will do, that the Father may be glorified in the Son. If you ask anything in *My name*, I will do it" (John 14:12–14).

Jesus casts a vision for powerful, far-reaching impact in the accomplishment of His mission. This is not a challenge to "out-sizzle" His works through some bizarre religious road show or televised fabrication of "miracles." This is a prediction of the global advancement of the gospel in the power of the Holy Spirit, whom He would send after His redemptive work and departure to heaven. And in the fullness of all that His name implies, He gives His disciples the key to confident prayer and lives that bring glory to God.

Asking in Jesus' Name

Jesus makes an authoritative guarantee. We all like guarantees. Advertisers tout "satisfaction guaranteed" and money-back guarantees on the products they want us to buy. Jesus, in the authority that only the Son of God can offer, makes a bold guarantee about prayer in this day and age. In John 14:13, Jesus says, "And whatever you ask in *My name,* that I will do, that the Father may be glorified in the Son." He keeps speaking of the power of His name in prayer in this upper room interaction.

In John 15:16–17, Christ expands our understanding of the necessity and proper use of His name, "You did not choose Me, but I chose you and appointed you that you should go and bear fruit, and that your fruit should remain, that whatever you ask the Father *in My name* He may give you."

In John 16:23–24, He states, "And in that day you will ask Me nothing. Most assuredly, I say to you, whatever you ask the Father in *My name* He will give you. Until now you have asked nothing in *My name.* Ask, and you will receive, that your joy may be full."

Misuse and Abuse

Today, we can find plenty of sad examples of the misuse and abuse of Jesus' name, both inside and outside the church. Recently, I did a simple YouTube search for the "funny" things we have done with the Lord's name in our prayers. One popular clip features a scene from the NASCAR comedy movie *Talladega Nights*, where the main character, a driver named Ricky Bobby, is leading a prayer for the family meal. (Incidentally, this is not an endorsement for the movie, as the scene is crude and sacrilegious—but is a cultural snapshot of the denigration of the idea of praying in Jesus' name.)

After opening his prayer by addressing God as "Dear Lord Baby Jesus," Ricky Bobby offers a superficial and slapstick gratitude for all the fast-food on the table and for each person present at the meal. Soon, Ricky Bobby's wife objects to the repeated "Baby Jesus" references, which ignites a debate around the table about how each person likes to "picture Jesus" as they pray. The ensuing discussion reveals a barrage of self-styled ideas about Jesus, picturing Him as a teenager, with a beard, in a tuxedo, a T-shirt, with wings, as a Ninja, and as the lead singer of a rock band. Ricky Bobby continues to pray, insisting on various descriptions of Jesus as a baby. The entire scene presents prayer as a joke and Jesus as someone we can define any way we want to as we use Him for our own entertainment and success.

This kind of nonsense and disrespect is not surprising coming from Hollywood and our pluralistic culture. However, Christians can sometimes be similarly superficial in the way we think of Jesus and use His name in our prayers. This should compel us to passionately embrace the biblical idea of praying in Jesus' name.

Condition and Result

So what was Jesus trying to help us understand? Really, He gives us a condition and result for all of our requests. The condition is that we ask in Jesus' name. Samuel Chadwick wrote, "To pray in the Name of Christ is to pray as one who is at one with Christ, whose mind is the mind of Christ, whose desires are the desires of Christ, and whose purpose is one with that of Christ." Chadwick further clarified, "Prayers offered in the Name of Christ are scrutinized and sanctified by His nature, His purpose, and His will. Prayer is endorsed by the Name when it is in harmony with the character, mind, desire, and purpose of the Name."[4] Clearly, Ricky Bobby didn't get this.

In his excellent book *The God Who Hears*, W. Bingham Hunter summarizes the New Testament teaching about praying in Jesus' name with these four truths:

- It seeks the glory of God.
- Its foundation is the death, resurrection, and intercession of Jesus.
- It is offered by Jesus' obedient disciples. (Hunter points out that praying in Jesus' name is virtually synonymous with obedience to Jesus.)
- It asks what Jesus himself would pray for.[5]

Hunter goes on to summarize: "The shortest and perhaps the best answer is simply: *Jesus prayed according to the will of God.*

And that, ultimately, is what it means for you and me to pray in Jesus' name—to pray according to the will of God."[6] This explains why Jesus was so emphatic that *whatever* we ask in *His name*, we will receive.

Dr. Randal Roberts of Western Seminary in Portland, Oregon, says, "It is to pray in a manner consistent with His values and purposes. . . . It is to pray with the glorification of God as the supreme motive; it is to pray as Jesus would pray were He in our circumstances; it is to pray as His followers who have been appointed as instruments of fruit-bearing in the outworking of His mission. . . . It is learning to ask for the good things that He delights to give from the devoted heart that He delights to bless."[7]

Holy-Name Dropping

In society, people have become accustomed to name dropping in order to get what they want. Mentioning a relationship with some powerful dignitary or popular icon can elicit admiration. People lacking the proper credentials will drop a name to gain access to an exclusive club or social gathering. Name dropping can get results in our superficial world that extols the rich and the famous.

Christians are not of this world. Our intentions and ambitions are focused on another kingdom. Yet in the most holy sense, Jesus' name produces results.

What happens when we pray in Jesus' name? What is the ultimate purpose and outcome? According to Jesus' multiple commands in this upper room discourse (John 13–17), the outcomes of praying in His name are:

- The Father will be glorified in the Son.
- We bear fruit that remains.
- Our joy is full.

How many times has prayer frustrated you rather than fulfilled you? Frustration comes from bombarding heaven with our own ideas of what God should do to accomplish our will in heaven. Fulfillment comes from knowing that His will is being implemented in our lives. Deep reward is found in knowing that the Father is glorified by our prayers and that our relationship with Him is producing the lasting fruit of deep character and spiritual impact. Joy comes from this deep fulfillment.

Frustration comes from bombarding heaven with our own ideas of what God should do to accomplish our will in heaven. Fulfillment comes from knowing that His will is being implemented in our lives.

John MacArthur notes that "biblical joy consists of the deep and abiding confidence that all is well regardless of circumstance and difficulty. It is the permanent possession of every believer—not a whimsical delight that comes and goes as chance offers it opportunity." He goes on to note that joy is "the flag that flies on the castle of the heart when the King is in residence."[8]

Getting It Right

Dale Carnegie was onto something. There are few things more uncomfortable than forgetting or mispronouncing someone's name. When someone does it to us, we care. Personally, I like to be called "Daniel" not "Dan." When someone calls me Dan, I tell them that the tribe of Dan was not an honorable group but that Daniel is one of my biblical heroes. Even in the small nuances, our names matter. The proper recollection and use of a name is vital in relationships.

Jesus' name matters when we converse with Him through prayer. When we get it right, He is honored and we are blessed. The real joy and assurance in prayer comes from the primary focus of seeking Christ's person and presence prior to His provision. Out of that intimacy of seeking His face, we discover again the wonder of His character, His heart, His purpose, and His will.

CHAPTER 12

How Revelation Motivates Our Response

People talk as if prayer is the way we get God to give us what we want.
Those who think this way seek prayer promises, techniques, locations,
mediators, and other methods they believe will influence God
or place Him under obligation.
But Scripture points in virtually the opposite direction, indicating prayer,
communication with the living God, as a means He uses
to give us what He knows we need.

W. BINGHAM HUNTER

I beseech you therefore, brethren, by the mercies of God,
that you present your bodies a living sacrifice,
holy, acceptable to God, which is your reasonable service.
And do not be conformed to this world,
but be transformed by the renewing of your mind,
that you may prove what is that good and acceptable and perfect will of
God.

THE APOSTLE PAUL—ROMANS 12:1–2

The excitement rose as we drove to the Richmond, Virginia, airport on a cool spring evening. We left right on time and my buddy Greg promised that he knew exactly how to get there. This was my first time to fly out of Richmond. Greg had been there many times and was confident we would arrive safely— and early.

I was in my first year of seminary and had an appointment the next day to interview Pastor John MacArthur, one of my ministry heroes, for a school project. Actually, I was going to interview several well-known Christian leaders while in California—but MacArthur was the first, and the one I was most excited about.

As we drove, we talked about our dreams for the future, joked a bit, and really were not watching the clock too closely. Suddenly Greg yelled, "What? How did we get here?" In our distraction, we had missed a key turn and had driven thirty minutes in the wrong direction. By the time Greg turned around and sped back to the airport, it was too late. I missed my plane and my interview with John MacArthur. To say the least, I was frustrated and disappointed. (In God's providence, I would eventually work for John MacArthur as his personal assistant and associate pastor—so I enjoyed many interviews, in time.)

Don't Miss This Turn!

I often say that worship is the response of all I am to the revelation of all He is. Revelation always requires a response. One of the amazing realities of worship-based prayer is the depth of response it evokes in our souls based on the revelation we pursue in God's Word as the beginning place of prayer. You do not want to miss the turn from all-embracing worship to all-consuming response. This is the elation of life change in the presence of God.

> *Worship is the response of all I am to the revelation of all He is. Revelation always requires a response.*

Indisputably, the book of Romans contains some of the most profound theology of the New Testament. The truths of Romans sparked Augustine's conversion, launched Martin Luther's reformation, and caused John Wesley's heart to be "strangely warmed" in a moment of life change.[1] The early church father Chrysostom would have the book of Romans read to him twice a week.[2] It has been called "the Constitution of the Christian Faith," the "Fort Knox of Bible doctrine," and even the "Fifth Gospel."

The first eleven chapters of Romans are packed with profound truths about God's saving and sanctifying work in Christ. This first section of the book climaxes in profound worship: "Oh, the depth of the riches both of the wisdom and knowledge of God! How unsearchable are His judgments and His ways past finding out! 'For who has known the mind of the Lord? Or who has become His counselor? Or who has first given to Him and it shall be repaid to him?' For of Him and through Him and to Him are all things, to whom be glory forever. Amen" (Romans 11:33–36).

Now, don't miss the turn that takes place in chapter 12. If you do, you will not reach your Christ-honoring destination. "I beseech you *therefore*, brethren, by the mercies of God, that you present your bodies a living sacrifice, holy, acceptable to God, which is your reasonable service. And do not be conformed to this world, but be transformed by the renewing of your mind, that you may prove what is that good and acceptable and perfect will of God" (vv. 1–2). The idea is clear. The response to all of this truth—the required acknowledgment of these great expressions of God's character and salvation plan—is sacrificial surrender to God and a renewed commitment to obedience to His will. This is the nature of all real spiritual growth and certainly core to transforming prayer.

Pictures of Profound Response

In the truest sense, a person cannot pray and remain the same. The commitment to seeking God's face in prayer, when properly understood and faithfully engaged, empowers personal change at the deepest level. I've seen it happen in the hearts of men who pray together from the Scriptures one morning each week. I've observed people receive a call to full-time vocational service in a moment of prayer. I have watched Spirit-prompted reconciliation occur in ways that years of dialogue and even counseling could not accomplish.

Changed in the Presence of the Unusual

My brother-in-law Vernon Brewer leads a nonprofit organization that specializes in providing practical aid and relief to other nations. As the founder and president of this organization for almost twenty years, he has traveled the world, collaborating with national leaders to provide Bibles, buildings, and vital supplies.

In January 2010, he traveled to Haiti, just two days after the massive 7.0 earthquake that devastated this island-nation, leaving some 220,000 dead and more than a million people displaced. During that week, he and his small band of co-workers slept in a tent in the backyard of a local pastor's home. In those days, they walked among the human wreckage, assessing and working to get immediate and long-term help in place.

Two days after his return from this initial trip, we ran into Vernon and his wife, Patti, at church. He was crying and unable to speak. Patti told us, "He has not stopped crying since he got back." As I sat next to him in the church services that morning, he broke down several times, weeping uncontrollably.

Vernon is no rookie when it comes to experiences of tragedy. He has been to over seventy nations. He later told me, "In my travels over the years, I have seen death. I have seen destruction. I have seen poverty. I have seen hopelessness. I have seen crime. I have smelled filth and decay. Never have I experienced all of these things with such intensity, all in one place. Haiti was unlike anything I have seen and felt." Vernon encountered the presence of unprecedented suffering, destruction, and death—and came home a changed man.

> When anyone is in the presence of something very powerful and unusual to their normal experience, it is difficult to remain the same.

When anyone is in the presence of something very powerful and unusual to their normal experience, it is difficult to remain the same. Prayer that begins with a pursuit of God's face, an encounter with His character, an experience of His presence—changes us at the deepest level. We must be aware of the Spirit and the Word working to help us make the turn of transformational response. Four common and essential responses are: a believing faith, authentic confession, conformity to His will, and empowerment for spiritual warfare.

His Face Evokes Our Faith

Imagine a couple married for sixty years. The wife has become ill and is on her deathbed. In a moment of unscripted candor, the wife shares some things that rivet her faithful mate. For sixty years, the husband made breakfast for his bride every day. He served up a consistent meal of eggs, toast, and juice. In her dying moment, the wife shares that she was never pleased with this breakfast. Her real desire was for oatmeal, fruit, and hot tea. The husband cannot believe it. Disappointment overwhelms his heart. "Why didn't you tell me?" The ailing wife responds, "You never asked what I wanted."

Like this strange dialogue of surprising displeasure, Christians can spend many years praying dutifully but never really please the Lord to whom they are praying. How? They are not praying in faith.

Hebrews 11:6 says, "But without faith it is impossible to please Him, for he who comes to God must believe that He is, and that He is a rewarder of those who diligently seek Him." Prayers that are not offered in genuine faith completely miss the mark of pleasing God's heart.

Worship-based prayer is a powerful spark that produces a response of faith. When we begin our prayers with a passionate pursuit of the character of God, we are gripped with the reality that "He is" and are soon reminded that "He is a rewarder of those who diligently seek Him." Again, notice the focus on "seeking Him," not just trying to solicit His help or provision. This is an emphasis on His face and a key to faith.

We are familiar with Romans 10:17, where it says, "So then faith comes by hearing, and hearing by the word of God." Scripture-fed, Spirit-led, worship-based prayer is the foundation that fills our minds with the truth of God's Word and great thoughts about God. We are then compelled to pray with a faith that becomes "the substance of things hoped for, the evidence of things not seen" (Hebrews 11:1). And He is pleased.

His Character Motivates Our Confession

Another very natural response in the presence of a holy God is genuine confession of the attitudes, actions, words, and intentions that are inconsistent with His character.

Confession means "agreeing with God" about our sin and failure to align with His person, purpose, and plan. First John 1:9 is so familiar yet empowering: "If we confess our sins, He is faithful and just to forgive us our sins and to cleanse us from all unrighteousness." When a genuine believer walks in the light and truth of Jesus, confession is the normal overflow of the heart. Yet there are those special times when profound awareness of God's character, truth, and presence pierces our heart deeply and evokes zealous confession.

Confessional Characters

One day King David looked down the long bony finger of the prophet Nathan as God used him to expose David's extended cover-up of adultery, murder, dishonesty, and pride. David's response is captured in Psalm 51, where he clearly looks past the truth-speaking Nathan and into the face of a holy God and cries, "Against You, You only, have I sinned, and done this evil in Your sight" (v. 4).

The prophet Isaiah encountered a vision of God "sitting on a throne, high and lifted up, and the train of His robe filled the temple" (Isaiah 6:1). Heavenly beings surrounded Him, declaring God's holiness as the temple shook and smoke poured forth. The prophet cried out, "Woe is me, for I am undone! Because I am a man of unclean lips, and I dwell in the midst of a people of unclean lips; for my eyes have seen the King, the Lord of hosts" (v. 5). The Lord cleansed Isaiah in response to his confession, and then called him to a far-reaching prophetic ministry. God's character of holiness led Isaiah to humility, confession, cleansing, and surrender.

Daniel was nearing almost seventy years in captivity when he was gripped by the truth found on the scroll of Jeremiah's prophecy that the time was very near for God's people to receive their liberation and return to Israel. In response, Daniel set his face to seek the Lord and worshiped the "great and awesome God, who keeps His covenant and mercy with those who love Him, and with those who keep His commandments" (Daniel 9:4). Then, in one of the most profound prayers of confession ever recorded in the Bible, he admits the great sins of God's people, longing for more than a return to the homeland—a return of God's glory to His people. His confession did not spring from comparing himself with the culture or with other people (we know Daniel was a blameless man), but in looking into the truth and face of God and becoming overwhelmed with the sinfulness of man.

The apostle Peter witnessed the power of Christ to overrule nature and trump Peter's skepticism. What the expert fisherman could not do with his expertise and experience during a full night of fishing, Jesus did with a single command. By His word, Christ filled multiple boats with a profound catch. Peter's response was to fall down at Jesus' knees saying, "Depart from me, for I am a sinful man, O Lord!" (Luke 5:8).

Lasting Restoration

One of the many ways I have seen this truth on dramatic display is at prayer summits. These multi-day "worship fests" are marked by spontaneous Scripture reading, singing, and heartfelt response, bringing people into an encounter with the living Christ that is incredibly intimate and moving. The more the truth of the Scriptures is read, heard, cherished, and applied—the more deeply the Spirit begins to expose needs, habitual sin, and broken relationships. Partway through a summit, we gather in smaller gender-specific groups.

The more the truth of the Scriptures is read, heard, cherished, and applied—the more deeply the Spirit begins to expose needs, habitual sin, and broken relationships.

Hearts open up as participants feel compelled to embrace the command of James 5:16: "Confess your trespasses to one another, and pray for one another, that you may be healed. The effective, fervent prayer of a righteous man avails much." I have seen hundreds of people restored to their first love for Christ and set free by His power through the confession that comes because of prolonged, powerful, worship-based prayer.

Confession that results from "getting caught" will be as deep as the negative consequences are enduring. Confession that comes because of some kind of peer pressure or group culture will be as lasting as the influence of the people involved. Confession that springs from worship, an encounter with the presence of the living God, will remain as long as God's character remains central.

A. W. Tozer described this reality: "The man who has struggled to purify himself and has had nothing but repeated failures will experience real relief when he stops tinkering with his soul and looks away to the perfect One. While he looks at Christ, the very things he has so long been trying to do will be getting done within him. It will be God working in him to will and to do."[3]

Our Wonder Leads to His Will

My wife and I have a living trust, which is a beefed-up version of a will. Creating this document was taxing and emotional, as we had to dig deep to figure out what our real wishes are for the things we own and the people we love. Lawyers will not allow you and I to complete anyone else's will, only our own, because a will is a specific and intimate expression of the wishes of the heart.

Our Lord and Master has a will. It is the specific and intimate expression of His heart. His Word is His will. The application is revealed by His Spirit. Our requests that have not been surrendered to His Word and Spirit in intimate pursuit may simply reflect our will, not His. Thus our clarity and confidence about the effect of our prayers will be clouded. Yet when our intent is clear and consecrated—"Your kingdom come, Your will be done"—we have confidence. Knowing His will comes from knowing Him, not just passing a list under His watchful eye.

First John 5:14–15 is another guideline for our requests: "Now this is the confidence that we have in Him, that if we ask anything according to His will, He hears us. And if we know that He hears us, whatever we ask, we know that we have the petitions that we have asked of Him." The Lord wants us to pray with authentic confidence. When our requests are clearly aligned and aimed at God's will, we have an assurance that is the goal for every believer. Put simply, His will is His Word, and when we learn to pray from the Scriptures in the Spirit-empowered personal abandon of worship, we are in a position to think clearly about His truth so it can shape all that we think, desire, and request.

Our Worship Empowers Our Warfare

Worship-based prayer infuses us with empowerment for the warfare zone we exist in every day of our lives. Word-infused prayer makes us ready to face spiritual enemies with "It is written" on our lips. Spirit-led prayer allows us to make application of truth to the challenges of the day and weakness of our flesh. We are on the winning team. All the provisions for conquering in life are abundant and available in Christ. Prayer is vital to our daily triumph and awakens us to the necessity of entering battle with a clear mission plan.

John Piper describes it well: "The number one reason why prayer malfunctions in the hands of believers is that they try to turn a wartime walkie-talkie into a domestic intercom. Until you believe that life is war, you cannot know what prayer is for. Prayer is for the accomplishment of a wartime mission."[4]

Warfare Made Simple

Many who write about spiritual warfare seem to think that we must be astute in a variety of extra-biblical tactics and special insights about the names and addresses of demons. Some people promote grandiose sketches of the evil hierarchy and fascinating geographical exposés of their organizational battle plan. It seems that a few special writers and researchers have developed the mystical formulas that the rest of us must learn in order to survive the struggles with the unseen world. To do this, we must buy their books, watch their DVDs, and attend their courses!

I may be naïve compared to the warfare experts, but I have discovered that a life of passionate worship—one that delights in biblical truth about God's character, seeks the empowerment of the Spirit for application and articulation, then surrenders in every way as prompted by this intimate encounter, is equipped to "fight the good fight" every day. Jesus, on the heels of forty days of prayer and fasting, wielded the truth of God's Word in facing down the devil in the wilderness (Matthew 4:4–11). We, too, are equipped by His sufficiency to brandish the "sword of the Spirit," which is the spoken word of God (Ephesians 6:17). We have His perfection and power living in us. He has given us the victory in His finished work of redemption. As we abide in Him, with hearts fully responsive to His intimate revelation of truth and insight, we overcome temptation and are delivered from evil.

> *As we abide in Him, with hearts fully responsive to His intimate revelation of truth and insight, we overcome temptation and are delivered from evil.*

A Small Minority With Supernatural Momentum

The province of Quebec is the least-evangelized region of the Americas. According to studies, less than 1 percent is evangelical in this very secular and nominal Catholic culture.[5] Since 1974, SEMBEQ,[6] a theologically conservative evangelical seminary in Montreal, has worked aggressively to disciple church leaders and plant new congregations. Ten years ago, they were exposed to the principles of worship-based prayer.

Francois Turcotte, a dynamic young pastor and emerging leader for the seminary, tells of his own reformation in prayer: "Even though I was a pastor, my prayer life was dull. I had more questions than answers, wondering if I was praying correctly or about the right things. Worship-based prayer opened up a completely new understanding. Prayer became a fresh and lifelong discovery of seeking His face, not just His hand. As we continued to learn and engage in seeking God, things began to change as the Lord compelled us to obedient response.

"In my own church we set aside a week of focused prayer and a fall prayer retreat. These fueled a deeper love for Christ, a strong unity, and greater passion for the lost. Around the region, in our association of pastors, we saw a dramatic change. Our pastors now begin their annual retreat with a full morning of Scripture-fed prayer, following the leadership of the Holy Spirit. The board of the seminary now spends the entire first day of our annual meetings in prayer, with very fruitful results in our unity and clarity about God's direction for the ministry. Several of us go away two times a year for a multi-day retreat of fasting, silence, the Word, and prayer. It has made the difference in our walk with Christ, our marriages, and our ministries. In addition, all the pastors of our association set aside an annual thirty-hour prayer time, where we simply seek the Lord and respond to His leadership in fresh surrender and ministry to one another."

Francois Picard directs the seminary and has seen the dramatic change in the lives and impact of their pastors. "In one of our early prayer gatherings, the Lord spoke to us with deep conviction about our lack of humility," Picard says. "With tears, pastors repented of their arrogance toward one another over past accomplishments and negative attitudes toward other ministries. Tears and brokenness have become common." He gives God glory for this work. "Before we tasted this awakening of prayer, we felt we were drowning, as we were so overwhelmed with the opposition to our work and wear from laboring in our own energy. We were tired of depending on new strategies and human wisdom. In the presence of God, we confessed that we had nothing in ourselves. Self-effort had failed."

Today, Picard notes, "Now it is more than 'opening' and 'closing' in prayer. We have been transformed by the impact of the Holy Spirit touching our hearts and are seeing renewed health and fresh fruit in our efforts in this mission field."

Turns Ahead

In the next section we will speak very practically about the methodology of worship-based prayer. The promise of transformation is applied when we engage in the reality of seeking God's face. Don't miss the turn. Revelation produces response. Response fuels confession, understanding of God's will, engagement in the battle, and fresh power for the mission. Everything is at stake. Let's proceed together.

Hearts Set Free:
A Trophy of Transformation

Many of us know the promises about spiritual freedom. Jesus said, "You shall know the truth, and the truth shall make you free" (John 8:32). Still, many praying Christians lug around chains of bondage that contradict their freedom and limit their joy.

Anne Neubauer, a respected wife, homemaker, and women's leader in her church, remembers well what happened when she and fellow believers began to focus on God's worthiness in prayer. "Together, the eyes of our hearts became fixed on the Lord and not on our list of needs," she says.

A specific freedom began to come into Anne's life. "He overwhelmed me with His love, presence, and joy to the point that I have been forever changed. The Lord completely healed my heart from the wounds I bore for so long and set me free from the lies I believed for many years. God has brought me to greater maturity through deep dependence on the truth, worth, and beauty of Jesus rather than on my performance as a believer. He revealed my calling to simply lead women to the throne of grace." From this position of freedom, God has fulfilled her desire to lead others to this reality.

"My husband and I have opened our home for prayer gatherings," Anne says. "We have also experienced great joy by serving together at several prayer retreats, where I have witnessed God restore marriages, repair broken relationships, reestablish hope, lift burdens, heal broken hearts, give needed wisdom and understanding, reveal callings, provide an organ for transplant, refresh weary hearts, fulfill desires for greater intimacy with Him, and so much more."

Anne's story reminds us that prayer is more than a rehearsal of temporal needs, but an avenue where we are changed and called to become change agents. She says, "Over the years, I have been blessed to see God faithfully reward those who seek Him. I can't imagine what heaven will be like worshiping Him together, but now I have a taste of it!"

PART THREE

CHANGE STARTS HERE

CHAPTER 13

Pray This, Not That

This prayer is a pattern for all Christian praying;
Jesus is teaching that prayer will be acceptable when, and only when,
the attitudes, thoughts, and desires expressed fit this pattern.
That is to say: Every prayer of ours should be
a praying of the Lord's Prayer in some shape or form.
We never get beyond this prayer.
Not only is it the Lord's first lesson in praying,
it is all the other lessons too.

J. I. PACKER

And take . . . the sword of the Spirit, which is the word of God;
praying always with all prayer and supplication in the Spirit,
being watchful to this end with all perseverance
and supplication for all the saints.

THE APOSTLE PAUL—EPHESIANS 6:17–18

David Zinczenko was once an overweight child. Today he is a leading expert on health and fitness, working as editor-in-chief of *Men's Health* magazine and editorial director of *Women's Health* magazine. He is also the author of numerous *New York Times* bestsellers, including a series of books based on his blockbuster hit *Eat This, Not That!* which exposed the caloric content and nutritional values of foods typically found in restaurants and grocery stores.

Americans spend an estimated $400 billion dollars a year eating out, according to Zinczenko, so you can see why his books have become so popular. People enjoy their food and entertainment, but many want to be healthy in the process. And these books are said to have helped millions attain that goal.

Jesus Helps Millions Pray

Every day millions of people pray in some form or fashion. Every day Jesus offers the truth and tools to help us do it effectively. In a real sense, He says, "Pray this, not that." His teaching is contained in the all-time bestseller, the Bible, which is the true owner's manual for life. The One who invented prayer tells us how to do it.

In Matthew 6:9–13, the Lord's Prayer, Jesus delivers the all-time final word on how *not to* pray—and how *to* pray. As multitudes flocked to hear Him on the hillside, His words resonated with unparalleled authority and practical application. For over two centuries, this prayer has equipped countless lives for real transformation.

In this sermon, Jesus exposed much of the superficial religious system of the day. In terms of their spiritual activities, He tells them what not to do in their giving, praying, and fasting. His words about giving and fasting are limited and primarily focused on what they should stop doing. His instruction on prayer balances the negative and the positive, with the bulk of the content dedicated to a positive model that applies to every generation.

In *Jesus' Pattern of Prayer,* John MacArthur writes, "Because communion with God is so vital, the enemy seems constantly to introduce errors into the church's understanding of prayer. Every generation at every time faces the necessity to purify a corrupted or confused comprehension of prayer."[1] In a sense, much of this book is intended to help us evaluate the ways we have been praying and align them more directly with clear biblical teaching. We do not want to be satisfied with a "corrupted or confused comprehension of prayer" in any sense.

Jesus exercised precision to dismantle the flawed view of

prayer common in His day. At their core, these errors still stalk us in our attempts to pray. We can easily get off course in our motives and our methods of prayer.

Don't Pray With Impure Motives

Jesus said, "And when you pray, you shall not be like the hypocrites. For they love to pray standing in the synagogues and on the corners of the streets, that they may be seen by men. Assuredly, I say to you, they have their reward" (Matthew 6:5).

When prayer becomes a religious exercise rather than a relational experience, it is formalized and convoluted, as was the case with the Pharisees of Jesus' day. It became a parade of religious stature and, as such, was proudly exhibited before the watching eyes of the adoring followers.

Jesus did not mean here that it is wrong to pray in a group or public setting. He did say that if your motive is to impress people, you'd better enjoy the moment, because that motive did not make the grade for eternal reward. Rather, Jesus told His followers to recognize that their Father saw them "in secret." Not only was this a reminder that God looks on the heart rather than the outward appearance, it compelled the disciples to gather in the privacy of an upper room rather than some venue for public consumption.

Don't Pray Using Ineffective Methods

Jesus turned His attention to another misguided group: the Gentiles. These were non-Jewish people, also known as heathen, who did not know, or pray to, the God of Israel. Jesus said of them, "And when you pray, do not use vain repetitions as the heathen do. For they think that they will be heard for their many words" (Matthew 6:7).

At the root of this wrong approach to prayer was a *flawed view of God*. The heathen apparently believed that their god was distant, impressed by religious performance and a bit temperamental in deciding to respond to their prayers. Their gods were in need of the persuasion of human prayers and seemed to require much coercion to act.

Accordingly, we see here that prayer is not about *a manipulation of words*. The heathen believed that their gods required many words, repeated phrases, and much persuasion flowing from religious fervor in order to grant favor and blessing. This reminds us of the prophets of Baal, who entered into a religious contest with the prophet Elijah (1 Kings 18:25–29), repeating their injunction all day long, jumping up and down on the altar and even cutting themselves to get the attention of their god— but with no results.

In a similar spirit, some today repeat the Lord's Prayer verbatim as some kind of magical charm. Jesus' intention was not that we simply recite this prayer to manipulate some blessing. It is not a celestial secret password to opening the treasuries of eternity. When I was in public high school, our football team quoted the Lord's Prayer together in the locker room before every game (back when this was legal). Maybe the coach saw it as some evangelism effort. For most of the players it was a superstitious ritual in hopes that God, whoever they conceived Him to be, would keep the team from serious injury and allow us to win the contest. After the game, half the team went out to a drunken party.

Our Father is completely dialed-in and capable. He is all-knowing and sovereign. He does not need the persuasion of our words or vigorous religious performances in order to know and meet our needs.

Of course, Jesus counters, "Do not be like them. For your Father knows the things you have need of before you ask Him" (Matthew 6:8). According to our Lord's words here, our Father is completely dialed-in and capable. He is all-knowing and sovereign. He does not need the persuasion of our words or vigorous religious performances in order to know and meet our needs. Further, the pattern of prayer He gives starts with the recognition of our "Father in heaven" and is very brief in the actual words employed.

Motivational Mistakes

In the next chapter we are going to unpack some direct and practical application of the pattern Jesus gave us, showing how we can use it to pray from the Scriptures. First, though, let's examine our own motivations and methods.

As much as we do not like to admit it, we can be a lot like the Pharisees of Jesus' day. It is easy to be caught up in our own religious activities and the familiar bubble of a "Christian culture" and go through the motions with convoluted motives. Like it or not, we are a performance-oriented society, and the church is just as bad, if not worse in some ways, as the world. The "performers" who really know how to produce and put on a good show of talent and entertainment are the headliners at most Christian gatherings. They may be pastors, authors, musicians, comedians, businessmen, or just ordinary people with a sizzling story. Either way you cut it, sizzle sells over substance.

So now we talk about prayer. Yes, holy and intimate as it is, the infection of pride and performance spreads even into our time with God. Over the years, I have known my own struggles with embracing the pure and persevering motives for prayer. I talk about this extensively in one of my previous books, *Fresh Encounters,* but want to review the potential pitfalls here. In my own journey and evaluation, I have concluded that some of our tainted motives are:

Guilt—the belief that if I do not pray, I will not be an acceptable Christian. Of course, no one wants another person to spend time with him or her simply to avoid or alleviate guilt. The Lord is no different.

Approval—the belief that if I do pray, I will be an acceptable Christian in the eyes of others. This was the flaw of the Pharisees. It is our belief that if we pray, and make sure others know we have done so, we will be good Christians—or good parents, or deacons, elders, or pastors in the church. This is the wrong approach for the wrong audience.

Church growth—the belief that prayer can be a useful tool to meet my tangible ministry goals. I often tell the story of hearing Pastor Peter Lord speak on this. He asked a group of aspiring ministry students: "If God promised you two things: (1) You would go to heaven when you die, and (2) He will never use you in the ministry again—would you still pray?" This pierced my heart because I knew my own tendency to pray so that God would use me—for *me*. God will not reduce something as pure as prayer to my next ego-driven church-growth tactic.

Revival—the belief that God will bring revival if I will just "work Him" enough through prayer. Of course, we all long for and desperately need revival. A few years ago, I heard a friend say, "There is a difference between seeking revival from God and seeking God for revival." Most of us long for revival—we just hope it starts in our denomination (not in that weird group down the road). Here is a key question: If a great revival came and then subsided, would we still be praying with the same passion *after* the revival as we did before? This made me wonder if there was a motive that was deeper and lasting, with or without revival.

The Enduring Motive

Graciously, the Lord has taught me that the only enduring motive for prayer is that God is worthy to be sought. Again, this is a worship-based motivation. I may or may not feel like praying. The prayer time may be energized; it may be dull. The answers to prayer may be apparent; they may not. Still, God is worthy to be sought.

I point out when I teach on this subject that worship-based prayer is eternal. In heaven, we will not confess, intercede, or engage in spiritual warfare. We will declare forever, "Worthy is the Lamb who was slain to receive power and riches and wisdom, and strength and honor and glory and blessing!" (Revelation 5:12). It is good to get in practice for this forever expression while we are still here on earth.

> The only enduring motive for prayer is that God is worthy to be sought.

So we pray because God is worthy. But there is a second side to the motivational coin: I am needy. As I said earlier, prayerlessness is our declaration of independence from God. The heart of real prayer is, "Lord, I need you. I cannot do it on my own. I must seek you today." These two motivational elements are seen in Psalm 40:16–17: "Let all those who seek You rejoice and be glad in You; let such as love Your salvation say continually, 'The Lord be magnified!' But I am poor and needy; yet the Lord thinks upon me. You are my help and my deliverer; do not delay, O my God."

Too often we can do all the right things for all the wrong reasons. You do not want to finish this book and launch off on another methodology of prayer. You need an enduring *why* to help you effectively learn *how*. I heard a speaker say once, "You can tell someone how to do something and they may keep it up for awhile. But if you show them why they are doing it—it will take a brick wall to stop them."

God is worthy. We are needy. We must pray with consistency and passion—until we take our last breath.

Adjusting the Approach

In reviewing Jesus' words about the Pharisees, I think we realize that our own traditions and bad theology can also land us in a rut of prayer that just does not work. Many Christians are as frustrated as the "heathen on the hill," struggling to find an approach that makes their walk with God real, natural, and sustainable for a lifetime.

So as we prepare to clearly understand and apply a pattern that can enliven our prayer life and give us a biblical, balanced approach to prayer, let's review a quick list of "pray this, not that" principles:

- Pray to seek God's face, NOT just His hand.
- Pray with your heart fixed on God's glory, NOT just for personal satisfaction.
- Pray from the treasury of God's Word, NOT from a list of your own ideas.
- Pray according to the Spirit's instruction, NOT only from human reason.

- Pray with a heart completely surrendered to His will, NOT with a hurried personal agenda.
- Pray in anticipation of living triumphantly in the war zone, NOT in satisfaction with your comfort zone.
- Pray that God would change *you*, NOT simply change *things*.

A Relationship, Not a Recipe

I assure you that an approach of worship-based prayer will open new windows of understanding about real intimacy with God. I believe it will empower your life for God's glory and your practical good.

In the next chapter we will look at a biblical, balanced pattern for practicing prayer. Still, I want to balance my enthusiasm, and all that you have read and will read in this book, with a needed perspective from Dr. J. I. Packer:

> *Each Christian's prayer life, like every good marriage, has in it common factors about which one can generalize and also uniquenesses which no other Christian's prayer life will quite match. You are you, and I am I, and we must each find our own way with God, and there is no recipe for prayer that can work for us like a handyman's do-it-yourself manual or cookery book, where the claim is that if you follow the instruction you can't go wrong. Praying is not like carpentry or cookery; it is the active exercise of a personal relationship, a kind of friendship, with the living God and his Son Jesus Christ, and the way it goes is more under divine control than under ours. Books on prayer, like marriage manuals, are not to be treated with slavish superstition, as if perfection of technique is the answer to all difficulties; their purpose, rather, is to suggest things to try. But as in other close relationships, so in prayer: You have to find out by trial and error what is right for you, and you learn to pray by praying.[2]*

Hopefully, the truth, testimonies, and living trophies of changed lives in this book are giving you the motivation and tools you need for transforming prayer. Ultimately, you will have to find your own way as you learn to pray by praying.

A Titanic Shift:
A Trophy of Transformation

Our churches are filled with people from every walk of life. Some of these people have high-powered jobs that demand long hours, engender significant stress, and leave them isolated from others. It is not their intention, but it happens.

Gary is an executive of a growing company that produces packaging for a variety of large retailers across the globe. You would recognize their packages on products from places like L.L. Bean, 3M, Costco, and many grocery stores. They even produce many of the mailing packages for the U.S. Postal Service.

One weekend, Gary made a sacrificial and, some might say, radical choice to go away with a group of men for a weekend retreat. He left his executive office in the company's 375,000-square-foot headquarters to attend a men's prayer gathering. While Gary loved the Lord and often prayed about many things in his life, this experience completely changed his understanding about prayer and connected him with other men at a profoundly deep level.

He testifies, "Remarkably, the concept of seeking God's face instead of His hand was a revelation. Praying in praise of who He is and not simply what He supplies was, amazingly, a titanic shift. The innate gratitude I had felt for so long, but never found expression, suddenly had meaning."

Gary says his life, family, and ministry have all been powerfully enriched by this transformation in his praying. "Worship-based prayer ignites a transparency between people so that they are able to share joys and burdens in a wonderfully profound way. Joy, peace, and fulfillment from being with the Savior and His people always results from worship-based prayer."

It is easy to be too busy to pray. Gary now understands that he is too busy not to pray, because He needs the refreshment of God's presence and the deep transparent fellowship of other believers. Like Gary, we have to take the risk and make the time to give the Lord our undivided attention. In that resolve we might just experience a titanic shift.

CHAPTER 14

Transforming Prayer for Dummies

Prayer is not asking God to do my will.
It is bringing myself into conformity with His will.
It is asking Him to do His will
and to give me the grace to enjoy it.

JOHN MACARTHUR

For of Him and through Him and to Him are all things,
to whom be glory forever. Amen.
I beseech you therefore, brethren, by the mercies of God,
that you present your bodies a living sacrifice,
holy, acceptable to God, which is your reasonable service.
And do not be conformed to this world,
but be transformed by the renewing of your mind,
that you may prove what is that good and acceptable
and perfect will of God.

THE APOSTLE PAUL—ROMANS 11:36–12:2

Few subjects and biblical texts have inspired more profound and deep sermon series and books than the Lord's Prayer, as we are accustomed to calling it. Personally, I have taught verse-by-verse, line-by-line through this passage on numerous occasions, seeking to deliver rich insight on the background, word meanings, cross references, and various applications.

Hopefully, my congregations have been inspired and helped. I know I have.

Concerning the Lord's Prayer, John MacArthur writes:

> *One of the marvels of the infinite mind of God is His ability to speak of vast themes in a few words. . . . No set of volumes, no exhaustive themes of great length, no series of teaching or preaching offered by men could ever have captured the fullness of what prayer is, and is to be, as does that profoundly simple model. It sets the standard for all praying. It encompasses all elements in prayer. It's for you, to change your prayer—and more, to change your life.*[1]

The Lord's Prayer is the ultimate pattern of prayer Jesus gave to His disciples. He repeated it twice in the gospels. The first delivery (Matthew 6) occurred near Galilee before a large crowd in the context of an extended sermon. His second iteration (Luke 11) occurred near Jerusalem after the disciples observed Him in prayer. He repeated this specific pattern after they made a request to learn how to pray.

He is worthy. I am needy. He is my all-sufficient, holy, and sovereign Father. I am His humble, weak, and dependent child. When these two realities meet, prayer transpires.

In one of the simplest analyses, we find that the Lord's Prayer has two main components.[2] The first section is about God's glory ("Hallowed be Your name. Your kingdom come. Your will be done"). The second part deals with man's need ("Give us day by day our daily bread. Forgive us our sins; do not lead us into temptation" [Luke 11]). Again, this is the heart of all prayer. He is worthy. I am needy. He is my all-sufficient, holy, and sovereign Father. I am His humble, weak, and dependent child. When these two realities meet, prayer transpires.

Many amazing books are available for in-depth study of the Lord's Prayer, and I encourage you to digest them eagerly and often.[3] But in this chapter, I am going to share an easy, memorable, and applicable tool you can use at any time to pray the essence of this prayer.

Simple and Applicable

In our information age, complexity abounds. Noise pollutes our yearning for spiritual equilibrium and simplicity. E-mails, text messages, tweets, and Facebook clutter our lives with more than we can possibly digest in any given day. Clear answers are often buried in a sea of tangential information and advertising found in books, magazines, the Internet, or the media.

Perhaps that is why the FOR DUMMIES book series is one of the strongest and most instantly identifiable brands in publishing. With more than 200 million books in print and more than 1,600 titles, the "Dummies" books do their best to present often complex subjects in plain English.

The Lord's Prayer is not complex, but in the mid-nineties I discovered a simple way to understand and implement this incredible prayer throughout my prayer life. I call it the "For Dummies" version because is it so simple and immediately applicable—and memorable. It has become a standard approach for my personal prayers.

I have also taught this pattern of prayer to thousands of pastors, prayer leaders, and church members. In my book *Fresh Encounters*, I demonstrate how it can be used to lead group prayer times. In another book, *PRAYzing!*, I showed how the pattern sparks a fresh creativity in prayer. Here, I want to help you understand its application in your personal prayer life. I hope to spark in you a worship-based approach in seeking God's face, then trusting Him for the vital issues of your journey.

The 4/4 Pattern

I grew up with a love for music. I played a couple of instruments, sang in high school all-state choirs, and received a scholarship for vocal music for two of my four years of college. So it was natural that I experienced a convergence between my love for the Lord's Prayer and my love for music. The result is what I call the "4/4 pattern" of prayer.

In music, the 4/4 pattern is the most basic beat. In adapting the elements of that pattern to the Lord's Prayer, it looks like this:

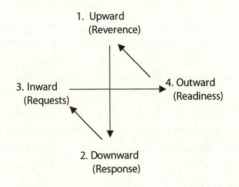

Every time I look at a biblical text as a springboard to prayer, I think in terms of this pattern. It is almost as if this diagram is engraved on my bifocals. As you think about this pattern, keep in mind that our prayers begin in the Scriptures. So I always start with an open Bible. Very often I use a Psalm—but really any text of God's Word can initiate our praying, using this pattern. We also know that our teacher is the Holy Spirit. We come to the text with a ready mind, but also with our entire being entirely surrendered to the instruction of the Holy Spirit as we pray.

↑ The Starting Place: Reverence

Imagine a conductor before an orchestra. The conductor raises a hand and fixes it high to capture the attention of the musicians. Every member is at full attention. In the prayer pattern Jesus gave His disciples, He instructs us to begin with *reverence*, an upward focus of worship ("Our Father in heaven, hallowed be Your name"). In keeping with Jesus' instructions, prayer begins with the character of God as we take time to focus our entire being on the wonders of who God is.

As our Father, He is caring and intimate. As the One who is in heaven, He is transcendent, holy, and separate. Striking this perfect balance, Jesus teaches us to draw near with assurance and awe, in heart-felt intimacy, holy imagination, and Abba adoration.

> *Jesus teaches us to draw near with assurance and awe, in heartfelt intimacy, holy imagination, and Abba adoration.*

Speaking of the priority of this first element of prayer, one writer says that this focus "calls for us to think about God, and in particular, His Name. Our prayers are to be suffused with large thoughts about God. We are to take the attributes of God, which are suggested by His various names. If our prayers are not focused on God, we are guilty of idolatry, as we are putting someone (or something) else in God's place."[4]

A. W. Tozer said it famously: "What comes to mind when we think about God is the most important thing about us . . . and the most portentous fact about any man is not what he at a given time may say or do, but what he in his deep heart conceives God to be like."[5] Spending quality time with an opened Bible, delighting in the names and character of God, is the most important engagement in our lives and the vital starting point of prayer. As we have discovered, this rivets our entire being on His name and sets our hearts on His glory as the goal of all prayer. This allows us to abide in Him as His Word abides in us. This brings us into conformity to the Lord Jesus so that we truly pray in His name.

Not only is our reverence a springboard to intimate, biblical, extended worship, but it is vital to the exercise of real faith in prayer. Hebrews 11:6 says, "But without faith it is impossible to please Him, for he who comes to God must believe that He is, and that He is a rewarder of those who diligently seek Him." Consider that all our praying may not please God if we do not pray in the faith that comes from the Word of God (Romans

10:17). This "upward" start puts our hearts in full attention and awe of who God is and assures us of His character and commitment to reward us as we set our hearts to seek Him, not just things from Him.

↓ The Downward Stroke: Response

Next, the musical conductor gives the downbeat and the composition begins. In this prayer pattern, our "music" of worship and praise has already commenced. Now we respond to God's character. Jesus taught the essence of this when He said, "Your kingdom come. Your will be done on earth as it is in heaven." This *response* to God's character in prayer involves yielding to the control of the Holy Spirit and recommitting ourselves to God's kingdom purposes. Introspection and surrender mark this time of yielding to the Spirit's promptings. It is a season of pledged obedience to the will and Word of God, desiring the accomplishment of His purposes in our lives.

Scottish writer Robert Law said, "Prayer is a mighty instrument, not for getting man's will done in heaven, but for getting God's will done on earth."[6] Warren Wiersbe explains that this moment of prayer involves "the devotion and dedication of our entire being to Jesus as we eagerly anticipate seeing him."[7] It involves praying with obedience and surrender to Jesus, who said, "Not My will, but Yours, be done" (Luke 22:42) for the sake of the Father's glory and kingdom purposes.

← The Inward Stroke: Requests

From the downbeat, the conductor now moves the baton, slanting upward and left, setting the tempo for the music. In prayer, we are now ready to express trust in God for the needs of our lives by way of our *requests*. I often say that we do not really know what to ask for until we have worshiped well and surrendered completely. Psalm 9:10 says, "Those who know Your name will put their trust in You." From this position of spiritual alignment, we come to the Father with our requests.

"Give us this day our daily bread. And forgive us our debts, as we forgive our debtors" (Matthew 6) invites us to pray about the *resource* and *relationship* issues of life. If we looked at the average prayer list, virtually every request would ultimately be a resource concern or a relationship concern. Jesus, in His divine wisdom, knew our journey and our struggles. This segment of trusting Him with a variety of inward matters allows us to lay it all out before Him.

> *If we looked at the average prayer list, virtually every request would ultimately be a resource concern or a relationship concern. Jesus, in His divine wisdom, knew our journey and our struggles.*

Praying about "daily bread" is more than hoping we can scrape some funds together to buy a fresh bagel at Panera Bread. This idea represents "all that we need to sustain life as we serve the Lord."[8] This is not a time of informing God of our needs, because He knows what we need before we ask (Matthew 6:8). Rather, this is an expression of conscious trust in God as the perfect definer and provider of our needs. It involves prayer about personal concerns, family and friends, daily circumstances, and even ministry matters.

Relationships matter to God. As the Word and Spirit are working in us, leading us into prayer "according to the will of God" (Romans 8:27), we will be compelled to evaluate our relationships to be sure that our conscience is clear and relationships are right (Acts 24:16).

We come to a place of relational alignment in this moment of prayer. This requires our confession of any sin that is revealed, leading to confession and restoration—both vertically (with the Lord) and horizontally (with others). Christians are a forgiven and forgiving people. This element of the prayer addresses the inward realities of our heart to align us with the heart of the One who is the God of self-sacrificing, gracious, merciful, and forgiving love.

→ The Outward Stroke: Readiness

As the music continues, the conductor moves the beat to the right, keeping tempo. As our prayer continues, the outward stroke reminds us of the spiritual contest before us and, more important, reassures us of the spiritual resources within us. We know the time comes when we must get off our knees and reenter the warfare zone. We must be battle ready.

When we pray, "Do not lead us into temptation, but deliver us from the evil one," we recognize our own inability to overcome the temptations and snares of daily life. We entrust our welfare for the warfare to the One who is our victor. Borrowing from the great spiritual combat text of Ephesians 6:10–20, we prepare our hearts and minds to "be strong in the Lord and in the power of His might" as we "put on the whole armor of God . . . to stand against the wiles of the devil" (vv. 10–11). In this moment of *readiness* for the battle, we affirm that "we do not wrestle against flesh and blood, but against principalities, against powers, against the rulers of the darkness of this age, against spiritual hosts of wickedness in the heavenly places" (v. 12).

We are praying to be battle ready through our trust in Christ. He is able to "make a way of escape" (1 Corinthians 10:13) and His Word is sufficient to equip us in the face of any temptation (see the example of Jesus in Matthew 4:2–11).

> *Prayer is not an escape from the battles of life but a great equipping to fight them in supernatural power.*

I often say the comfort zone is the danger zone. As we come to the concluding moments of a prayer time, we not only anticipate but also embrace the responsibility to "fight the good fight." We are called to be praying menaces to the devil. Prayer is not an escape from the battles of life but a great equipping to fight them in supernatural power. The very fact that we are seeking God's face and engaging in life-giving prayer alerts the enemy to our increased threat to his dominion. When we pray, we pick a fight with the devil at a completely new level. Yet this is why we are on earth—not to cruise along on a luxury liner until Jesus comes, but to stay actively engaged in our "search-and-rescue mission" in the midst of the global spiritual battle for the hearts and minds of people.

↑ The Upward Stroke: Reverence

With an upward motion, the conductor returns the beat to the starting point. The traditional version we recite (from the King James Version of Matthew 6:13), concludes on a high note of praise: "For thine is the kingdom, and the power, and the glory, for ever. Amen." We conclude our prayer with a doxology, an expression giving glory to God. We close the door on prayer the same way we opened it—with praise.

More Than a Five-Minute Prayer

Many Christians pray without a clear understanding of the foundational role of worship in prayer and lack a biblical, balanced model. As a result, they reduce their time with God to an abbreviated, dutiful routine that rehearses a few superficial topics, then moves into the activities of the day. Joe was one of those people.

Joe is a leader in his local congregation in Fond du Lac, Wisconsin. Recently, I spoke at a regional seminar sponsored by his church. Throughout the day, I could tell Joe was very engaged. His body language indicated "the lights were coming on" in a new way concerning his prayer life.

At the end of the day, Joe clarified what I had sensed. With tears, this strong, handsome church leader, husband, and father approached me. "Thank you," he said. "I've been changed today. All my life, I have only sought God's hand—seeking what He could give me or how He could help me. My heart has been riveted by the call to seek His face, first and foremost. I am feeling so compelled to understand this more and to seek Him solely because He is worthy to be sought. I'm tired of my five-minute-a-day prayer life. I so want to experience this kind of intimacy with Christ."

The next day, as I was speaking in the Sunday services, Joe tracked me down between the two worship hours and asked me to join him in a nearby empty classroom. With tears, Joe told me a story of a routine but profound experience he had following the seminar the night before. He had written it down. Pulling out a scribbled note, he read:

"Tonight when I went to feed our dog, Jackson, just like any other night, I walked to the kennel, opened it up, let him run to do his duty, and then went into the garage to get food to feed him. When I went back to the kennel, he was eagerly anticipating my food that I was going to give him. Like usual, I poured the food in his dish and stroked his head and ears. Then, when I went to close the kennel, I called him over and he nuzzled his head and chin in where I could pet him. The Lord prompted me, 'See how you like it when he comes over and seeks you and not the food.' I stopped and realized a profound truth!"

Joe's story is simple but reflects a discovery that changed the trajectory of his relationship with Christ. Of course, Joe delights in caring for and feeding his pet. However, even in this simple interchange with man's best friend, we see Joe's fresh awareness of the delight both he and the Lord feel when the relationship is prioritized in the midst of daily routine. Joe's prayer life changed from a five-minute check-in call to the joy of seeking God's face. I believe this is a change we all desire—and can experience. Now we want to see the practical reality of how it can happen every day.

Race Did Not Matter at the Foot of the Cross: A Trophy of Transformation

Many times in our lives, the Lord is accomplishing several things all at once in our hearts as we seek Him. On one level, He is teaching us more about himself and what it means to seek Him. On another level, He may be teaching us more about our own hearts or our situation that produces a powerful change in our lives and life direction.

Alice Moss has walked with the Lord for many years. As a women's Bible study leader, she began to integrate Bible study, prayer, and worship in leading the women. She says, "The experience left me feeling uplifted and joyful. I had no name for what we were doing, but I definitely knew I found something precious. It was the worship and prayer put together that made all the difference for me."

One day Alice was invited to attend an event that featured several days of worship-based prayer. Reflecting on this moment she writes, "God placed such a strong desire to attend within my heart that I could only obey. I didn't know what to expect and thought it strange there would be no speakers or musicians— just time spent with God. I remember thinking there is only so much prayer one could do at any given time."

But God had another story He was writing for Alice. "Being one of two African-Americans present at the gathering was not an issue. Race did not matter at the foot of the cross. In truth, it was there that I truly saw the body of Christ for what it is: people from every ethnicity giving worship and adoration to the only One who is worthy." God gave Alice a fresh vision of His face and a new appreciation of His body. "The Lord embraced me and enveloped me in His love that weekend and I have never been the same. His warmth, vitality, intimacy, and power were demonstrated to me over and over again until God captivated my heart, mind, spirit, and will. He filled me with the realization that He wanted a love-relationship with me and that I could have that intimate relationship simply by drawing near to Him in prayer."

Today the Lord is using Alice to share this passion in many

places around the world. She leads prayer events, trains hundreds every year in the principles of worship-based prayer, and is a featured speaker at the very popular "True Woman" conferences sponsored by radio teacher Nancy DeMoss.

In describing the fruit of her ministry, Alice shares, "I often hear from attendees how their lives have been transformed because they were ushered into God's presence through prayer. They leave excited, anxious to have me come and teach it to their churches and leaders.

"Worship-based prayer shifts our focus from our needs to His worthiness," Alice says. "Everything in life pales in comparison to the worthiness of God. As we begin to enlarge our vision of God's character rather than focusing only on what we want Him to do for us, He fulfills us in ways that cause us to want more of Him. Worshiping God, for *who* He is, creates an intimacy with Him and opens His hand where all needs are met."

When we give God our undivided attention, He is at work to change our hearts, our perspective, and the trajectory of our life. As Alice notes, "It lit a fire of delight and zeal in my heart for the Lord and keeps it burning to this day."

CHAPTER 15

This Is How We Do It

At the beginning of our Christian life
we are full of requests to God.
But then we find that God wants to get us into relationship with
Himself—
to get us in touch with His purposes.

OSWALD CHAMBERS

Now it came to pass,
as He was praying in a certain place,
when He ceased,
that one of His disciples said to Him,
"Lord, teach us to pray,
as John also taught his disciples."

LUKE 11:1

As already noted, over the years I have enjoyed the privilege of leading a variety of prayer experiences. Some have been for six hours; others three and a half days. We have gone away with small leadership teams and even enjoyed this format with groups of two hundred-plus.

In the course of this prayer journey, I have become captivated with the sufficiency of God *in* prayer and *for* prayer. Often, as people arrive for these extraordinary experiences (usually held at a camp or conference center), they wonder how in the world a group of people is going to pray for hours and days on end. The Lord is always faithful. As I say, "God is always glad to oblige when you give Him your undivided attention."

Of course, a request-based approach would typically run out of steam after twenty minutes, maybe an hour at best. But in the free-flowing dynamic of opening our Bibles, trusting the Spirit's leadership, and allowing all who feel prompted by the Spirit to participate—a full kaleidoscope of prayer options emerges.

I like to call it Christianity in its purest form, as there are no celebrity speakers, music groups, bulletins, or agendas. In fact, for me this is one of the most beautiful demonstrations of the sufficiency of the Word of God, the Spirit of God, and the people of God in active and practical ministry. My faith in God's desire and power to lead us into life-changing, Christ-exalting prayer has grown immensely over the years.

Bible Boogie Board—Holy Spirit Wave

As I travel and speak, it is this confidence that guides me as I engage in an experience I affectionately describe as "grabbing my Bible boogie board and catching the Holy Spirit wave." I lead the group through a process of spontaneously picking a psalm. After reading the psalm together, I lead the people "on the fly" through the steps of the 4/4 pattern, demonstrating how it kindles worship, springing from truths about God. Following a time of spontaneous worship, we then pray from the text with the focus on the other elements of this prayer pattern. The process is always a spiritual adrenaline rush but also so fresh and life giving.

So let's see how we can make this approach very practical. Again, we always begin with the Scriptures, and then I use four key questions to bring focus and stimulate specific prayers. I call these the *who, how, what,* and *where* questions of practicing this pattern.

- Who is God? (reverence)
- How should I respond? (response)
- What do I pray about? (requests)
- Where do I go from here? (readiness)

174

Reverence (the Starting Place): Who Is God?

Begin with a psalm or some other portion of Scripture. Because this is a worship-based approach, the first question as you read any passage of Scripture is: "Who is God?" Asked another way, "What does this passage reveal about God and His character?" Invite the Holy Spirit to give you understanding of what the text tells you about the Father, Son, and Holy Spirit.

The goal is to discover truths about God's nature, names, and person in the Bible text you are reading. Mark them in your Bible as you begin your prayer time. Alternatively, write out the list of these truths, with the corollary verses where they are found.

> The goal is to discover truths about God's nature, names, and person in the Bible text you are reading.

Then begin your prayer time seeking His face in worship, using your own words. You may utilize simple "finish the sentence" prayers like, "I praise you because you are . . ." Or you may focus on a particular attribute of God, like His power: "God, I have seen your power . . ."—then describe the ways He has made His power known to you. Or you might focus on His grace with a prayer that says, "Thank you for showing me your grace when . . ." Honor Him for the many indicators of His grace in your life.

The Holy Spirit can initiate a variety of ideas as you worship from the Word. Blend some songs in as well, based on the truths you discover about God. This time can take a significant amount of your prayer time—fifteen minutes or more. Sometimes, it becomes the entire focus of your prayer time. God is honored and all is well.

Response (the Downward Stroke): How Should I Respond?

Remember, revelation demands response. So how do you want God's kingdom to come and His will to be done in your life in response to His character? Using cues from the Scripture, you can pray, "Father, be Lord of my . . ." or "Lord, rule over . . ." You can submit specific dimensions of your life to His authority—like your mind, emotions, doubts, fears, plans, career, family, ministry, etc. Confess areas of your life that require fresh surrender to His will—like your thought life, friendships, marriage, finances, or children.

Punctuate this time with songs of surrender and humility. If you journal, reflect on what the Lord is putting into your heart during this time. Write specifically about your expressions of submission and yieldedness.

Requests (the Inward Stroke): What Should I Pray About?

Again, it is amazing how our frame of mind changes during the reverence and response segments, so that our time of bringing requests to the Lord is energized by faith and conducted with a passion for God's will and glory. If you have a prayer list, you can utilize it here. However, let the passages of Scripture guide you in the articulation of your requests.

Many times a passage will give you practical clues about how you can trust the Lord for the resources and relationships of your life. Maybe the Scripture you are using addresses the issue of fear. You begin to pray, "Lord, I will trust you for my fears about . . ." Or, you may pray for others, "I pray for _____ (name) as they cope with fear in the midst of _____ (situation)."

Perhaps the text speaks of various struggles, needs, decisions, challenges, or longings. Turn these into specific prayers of trust as you commit various resource concerns and arenas of relationships to the Lord. It is amazing to see how the Spirit will expose needs and direct your prayers according to the will of God.

Readiness (the Outward Stroke): Where Do I Go From Here?

Toward the end of the prayer time, thoughts tend to move toward the hours, days, or weeks that are before you. The "where?" question simply prompts you to think about the mission of your life and the warfare you can anticipate.

Many texts will speak of some challenge or spiritual enemy to overcome. These cues will guide you in identifying and anticipating practical spiritual battles. Just as Jesus used the memorized Word to defeat Satan, look for a promise or truth that you can pray over the temptations, toils, and snares that await you beyond the door of your prayer room.

Perhaps the text speaks of God's power over His enemies. You might pray, "Lord, I will rely on your power as I face the enemy, or challenge, of _____." Or perhaps there is a promise in the text. You might pray, "Be my victory as I encounter _____." Then quote that promise, repeatedly, as you list the battles you might face. It is a great way to integrate Scripture memory into your prayer time as you become battle ready.

Reverence (the Upward Stroke): Who Is God?

End where you began, with your eyes on Him. You have expressed your reverence in Scripture-fed, Spirit-led worship. You have responded in submission to His kingdom purposes and will. You have trusted Him with requests for the resource and relationship concerns of life. You cultivated readiness in your heart and mind for the battles ahead. Now, with your eyes on Him, declare, "For Yours is the kingdom and the power and the glory forever. Amen" (Matthew 6). This is a great moment to conclude with a song focused on His lordship, power, and glory.

Practical Models From the Living Word

Previously, I mentioned a prayer tool I use and enjoy. Since the mid-seventies *The 29:59 Plan* has sold over 600,000 copies, testifying to its usefulness.[1] One of the new features of this plan is a series of work sheets that walk you through the process of selecting a text from God's Word and using the 4/4 pattern to pray from that section of Scripture. I highly recommend it. For now, let's take a psalm, then a New Testament passage, and show how to put this pattern into play.

Psalm 46

1 God is our refuge and strength, a very present help in trouble.

2 Therefore we will not fear, even though the earth be removed, and though the mountains be carried into the midst of the sea;

3 Though its waters roar and be troubled, though the mountains shake with its swelling. Selah

4 There is a river whose streams shall make glad the city of God, the holy place of the tabernacle of the Most High.

5 God is in the midst of her, she shall not be moved; God shall help her, just at the break of dawn.

6 The nations raged, the kingdoms were moved; He uttered His voice, the earth melted.

7 The Lord of hosts is with us; the God of Jacob is our refuge. Selah

8 Come, behold the works of the Lord, who has made desolations in the earth.

9 He makes wars cease to the end of the earth; He breaks the bow and cuts the spear in two; He burns the chariot in the fire.

10 Be still, and know that I am God; I will be exalted among the nations, I will be exalted in the earth!

11 The Lord of hosts is with us; the God of Jacob is our refuge.

Reverence: Who Is God?

As you read and prayerfully extract truths about God, you will discover ideas like:

Refuge and strength—v. 1; All-present—v. 1; Helper in trouble—v. 1; Holy—v. 4; Most High—v. 4; Powerful (voice)—v.

6; Lord of Hosts—vv. 7, 11; With us—vv. 7, 11; Refuge—vv. 7, 11; Judges the earth—v. 8; Brings peace—v. 9; Defeats His enemies—v. 9; Exalted—v. 10.

Possible prayer prompters:

- I praise you, Lord, that you have been my refuge when . . .
- I praise you that you gave me strength when . . .
- I praise you that you are so strong, you can . . .
- I praise you that you have been (or are) present when . . .
- I praise you that you have helped me when I encountered the trouble of . . .

You get the idea. Turn the truths about God into a springboard of practical and specific expressions of worship or reverence. Notice the repeated truths in verses 7 and 11. Because of the double emphasis, you might want to focus on expressions like:

- I praise you that you are the Lord of Hosts, reigning today over . . .
- I praise you that you are with me when . . .
- I praise you that you are my refuge when . . .

Of course, you can incorporate a variety of hymns or other worship songs that relate to many of these truths about God. Sing to Him!

Response: How Should I Respond?

Revelation demands response. Based on the time of worship around the biblical themes and practical application of God's character, how might you respond? How can you submit to His kingdom purposes? How can you surrender your will to His? What passages might guide that response? Here are some ideas from Psalm 46:

- Lord, I confess and surrender my fears (v. 2) about. . . .
- Lord, I welcome your very present help (v. 5) in . . .

- Lord, I submit my thoughts and plans about _____
  to the power and authority of your voice (v. 6);
- Lord of Hosts (vv. 7, 11), rule over my . . .
- I submit my _____ (situation, thoughts,
  plans) to you. Help me to be still (stop striving, let go,
  relax) and seek your glory alone (v. 10).

What Should I Pray About?

From this experience of worship and position of surrender,
now you can pray from an abiding heart and in Jesus' name (as
Jesus would pray). Here are some requests in the two subcat-
egories of resources (daily bread) and relationships (forgiveness
and restoration):

Resources:

- I ask for a sense of security (v. 1) about . . .
- I ask for your strength (v. 1) in order to . . .
- I pray for your gladness and joy (v. 4) in the midst of . . .
- For _____ to see the "works of the Lord" (v. 8).

Relationships:

- I pray for your presence and help (v. 1) in _____
  (relationship).
- Because you "make wars cease" (v. 9), I ask you to work in
  _____ to bring peace and reconciliation.
- Help _____ to be still and know that you
  are God in his/her relationship with . . . (v. 10).

Readiness: Where Do I Go From Here?

As you prepare to enter the war zone and mission field, pray
about battles and struggles. Get ready to experience the Lord's
power and victory in these trials and temptations.

- I will trust in your presence and protection (vv. 7, 11)
  today as I . . .
- Because you are mighty in confronting your enemies
  (v. 9), I will trust you to overcome my struggle with . . .

Reverence: Who Is God?

Close with a "doxology" moment.

- You are exalted (v. 10) among . . .

Consider closing with a song of praise as you declare from your heart to His, "For Yours is the kingdom and the power and the glory forever. Amen."

1 Peter 5

Now let's look at a passage from the New Testament. Incidentally, you do not have to pray from an entire chapter. Select a portion that is substantive, yet short enough to work for you. I picked this passage randomly as it is one of the shorter chapters of the New Testament:

> 1 The elders who are among you I exhort, I who am a fellow elder and a witness of the sufferings of Christ, and also a partaker of the glory that will be revealed:
>
> 2 Shepherd the flock of God which is among you, serving as overseers, not by compulsion but willingly, not for dishonest gain but eagerly;
>
> 3 nor as being lords over those entrusted to you, but being examples to the flock;
>
> 4 and when the Chief Shepherd appears, you will receive the crown of glory that does not fade away.
>
> 5 Likewise you younger people, submit yourselves to your elders. Yes, all of you be submissive to one another, and be clothed with humility, for "God resists the proud, but gives grace to the humble."
>
> 6 Therefore humble yourselves under the mighty hand of God, that He may exalt you in due time,
>
> 7 casting all your care upon Him, for He cares for you.
>
> 8 Be sober, be vigilant; because your adversary the devil walks about like a roaring lion, seeking whom he may devour.
>
> 9 Resist him, steadfast in the faith, knowing that the

same sufferings are experienced by your brotherhood in the world.

10 But may the God of all grace, who called us to His eternal glory by Christ Jesus, after you have suffered a while, perfect, establish, strengthen, and settle you.

11 To Him be the glory and the dominion forever and ever. Amen.

12 By Silvanus, our faithful brother as I consider him, I have written to you briefly, exhorting and testifying that this is the true grace of God in which you stand.

13 She who is in Babylon, elect together with you, greets you; and so does Mark, my son.

14 Greet one another with a kiss of love. Peace to you all who are in Christ Jesus. Amen.

Reverence: Who Is God?

From this text you see that God is:

The suffering Savior—v. 1; God of glory, He lives in glory, He will reveal His glory; He will take us to glory—v. 1; He works in us to give us a willing heart—vv. 2–3; Chief Shepherd—v. 4; Rewarder—v. 4; Resists the proud—v. 5; Gives grace to the humble—v. 5; Mighty—v. 6; Exalts the humble—v. 6; Cares for us—v. 7; Gives us faith and power to resist the devil—v. 9; God of all grace—v. 10; Eternal—v. 10; Glorious—v. 10; Calls us—v. 10; Redeems our experiences of suffering—v. 10; Perfects, establishes, strengthens, settles—v. 10; Glorious—v. 11; Dominion and rule—v. 11; Gives us grace to stand—v. 12; God of peace—v. 14.

As you can see, there are many ways from this passage to say, "Father in heaven, hallowed be Your name." A few examples:

- I glorify you (vv. 1, 10, 11) because you are . . .
- I praise you that you have shown your grace (v. 5) . . .
- I worship you because your hand is mighty (v. 6) over . . .

Response: How Should I Respond?

Here are some possible prayers of surrender to His purposes and will:

- I surrender my attitudes of "compulsion" and duty (v. 2), asking you to make me willing to . . .
- I surrender my attitude of greed ("dishonest gain") (v. 2) in _____ (situation).
- Chief Shepherd (v. 4), I submit my _____ to your leadership and will trust you for your reward.
- Rule over my lack of submission and humility (vv. 5–6) in _____ (situation).
- Humble my pride of _____ under your mighty hand (v. 6).
- Even though it is hard, I embrace my suffering (v. 10) in _____ (situation).

Requests: What Should I Pray About?

Again, the Spirit would give you specific insight in the moment as to what you should pray about, but here are a few ideas:

Resources

- I cast my cares (v. 7) about _____ upon you, thanking you that you care for me.
- I pray for _____ as he/she encounters trials (sufferings—v. 10), asking that you would perfect, establish, strengthen, and settle him/her.

Relationships

- Help me to be an example (v. 3) to _____ (people) as I serve them willingly.
- Help _____ (name) to submit to you and to _____ (name) in his/her relationship.
- Give _____ (name) humility and grace (v. 5) as he/she deals with _____ (relationship).

Readiness: Where Do I Go From Here?

Themes about the spiritual battle are obvious in this text. A few prayer ideas include:

- Give me your grace to be sober/self-controlled and vigilant/alert as I face the enemy today in _____ (specific trials or temptations).
- Today, I will resist the devil's attacks and stand firm in my faith, through your promise of _____ (claim Scripture promises from this text or anywhere in the Bible; meditate on these promises in light of the battles of the day).

Reverence: Who Is God?

- Repeat the doxology (v. 11) several times with conviction!
- Praise Him for His peace (v. 14).
- Sing—"It Is Well With My Soul."

Seed Thoughts vs. Spirit Thoughts

The previous examples are just seed thoughts. The Spirit is the teacher, in the moment, in every moment of prayer. The Spirit takes the Word, making our worship soar and causing His Word to flourish in our prayers.

> *My hope is that in the simplicity of this pattern you also sense the sufficiency of the Word and Spirit in your praying and in your living.*

Again, the goal is not to train you in a new technique but to motivate you to a life of prayer, according to the teachings of Christ. My hope is that in the simplicity of this pattern you also sense the sufficiency of the Word and Spirit in your praying and in your living. The goal is that this kind of prayer is woven into the fabric of your life and that your life is woven into the fabric of your praying.

Note: This same approach works well in a small-group setting, inviting participants to join in with scriptural prayers, responses, and spontaneous singing as you provide direction from the Scriptures.

To implement a large-group prayer time, using instrumentation, PowerPoint, and other support tools, look for examples of the "Fresh Encounter" worship-based prayer formats on our Web site: *www.transformingprayerbook.com.*

Just Getting Warmed Up:
A Trophy of Transformation

Probably every Christian has battled distraction while trying to pray. Often, if we get a few minutes of focused prayer in before our mind wanders, we feel we are doing pretty well. The idea of praying for thirty minutes or even an hour seems almost impossible as we easily run out of things to say and struggle to keep on track.

Gary, a busy husband, father, and dentist knew this struggle for many years. "I was taught that prayer was part of a balanced Christian life. I didn't know exactly what *ask, seek,* and *knock* meant except that if I wanted something from God I could ask Him for it. I believed it was only the really good Christians who would stay up all night praying together."

As he reflects on his first experience of spending extended time in prayer with other believers, he notes, "I wanted to be part of what God was doing in our church. As a group, we spent the time in worship with singing, Scripture reading, meditation, and petition. In the midst of all this activity, God spoke very specifically to me as I participated. It was unlike anything I'd experienced before."

Today, Gary makes time in the midst of his busy life to enjoy extended times of prayer. He even leads a weekly prayer time and often helps facilitate prayer retreats. "I pray more often and for a longer duration," he says. "During the day, I am aware of a connection to God as I have learned to worship and pray anytime, anywhere. I've even begun reading the Bible more because many Scriptures are useful for praise and worship. My wife and I often pray together, and I have found that praying together builds a deeper relationship with others."

Christians who are frustrated with punctuated, distracted prayers can find hope in Gary's journey. As he describes it, "The passion Jesus expressed in the garden with His disciples before His crucifixion has always fascinated me. He pleaded with them to pray for just one hour. I would wonder, *That's a long time! How could I ever pray for a whole hour?* Today, with worship-based prayer, an hour goes by quickly and I find I am just getting warmed up! Glory to God!"

CHAPTER 16

Coming Out of the Prayer Closet

We have become a society of
solo sapiens.

LYLE SCHALLER

These all continued with one accord in prayer and supplication,
with the women and Mary the mother of Jesus, and with His brothers.

ACTS 1:14

Over two hundred people stood shoulder-to-shoulder, arm-in-arm, hand-in-hand, around a beautifully decorated Communion table. Tears flowed from radiant faces. Some looked heavenward while others worshiped with eyes closed. In angelic harmony, our voices resounded in the final verse of "All Hail the Power of Jesus' Name."

This moment felt as close to heaven as anything I had ever experienced—but I knew I wasn't there yet, just peeking over the precipice. We resonated with unleashed joy (changing the words to reflect our worship): "O that with yonder sacred throng we at *your* feet may fall. We'll join the everlasting song, and crown *you* Lord of All. We'll join the everlasting song, and crown *you* Lord of All." This was followed by the most powerful, passionate, harmonious, musical "Amen" I had ever heard, then five minutes of unleashed applause for the King of Kings and Lord of Lords. This moment of united prayer was as intimate, free flowing, and exhilarating as anything I've known in my entire Christian journey.

The evening began two hours earlier with a variety of Scripture readings and songs of praise flowing spontaneously from the hearts of people around the room. About thirty minutes into the meeting, the focus turned to verses and songs extolling Christ and His work on the cross. At a certain point, we invited participants to come to the table, in worthy fashion, with hearts pure and focused. Some came alone, others with their spouse, while still others grouped up for their time of remembering Christ's body and blood.

At the same time, around the periphery of this large room we had placed prayer stations where individuals could pray in interactive fashion, using a variety of visual tools and Scripture verses to enjoy the moment in intimate spiritual communion. Included in the stations were a couple of positions for foot washing for those who felt compelled to express their servant heart in this way. It was all a highly participatory experience of Word, worship, and encouraging fellowship.

As participants completed the extended time of communion, we rose from our chairs and drew together in close-knit fashion, standing in concentric circles around the table in a final series of *a cappella* songs. This was the culmination of this extraordinary Communion service, the ending of three days of unscripted Word and worship.

Every time I enjoy these experiences of extraordinary corporate prayer, I am reminded that transformation is not something that occurs only in privacy. It is also fueled by praying in community with others. I could not wrap up this book without a strong challenge to find transformational prayer in community to complement your personal prayer journey.

Individual + Community = Transformation

We know that God wants our prayers to be transformational. If you were to ask, "Which is more important, private prayer or corporate prayer?" My answer would always be "yes"! It is like asking which leg is more crucial to walking—the right or the left?

In the early church, they understood the value of community—meeting together daily in prayer and the other vital disciplines for spiritual growth. In Acts 2:42, we see the discipleship patterns that emerged immediately in the Jerusalem church, comprised almost entirely of new believers. It says, "And they continued steadfastly in the apostles' doctrine and fellowship, in the breaking of bread, and in prayers." You could *not* learn the apostles' doctrine by downloading a message to your iPod! You had to be gathered in community. The same was obviously true of fellowship and the breaking of bread. And how did they learn to pray? *Together.*

These prayers were not just a blessing tacked on to the beginning and end of a Bible study. These early Christians gathered exclusively for prayer. In all likelihood they followed the pattern Jesus set forth that led them through themes of worship, submission, intercession, supplication, warfare, and praise. In extended seasons of corporate prayer, they learned to pray effectively.

The church was birthed in a ten-day prayer meeting (Acts 1:14; 2:1). They coped with crisis and persecution together, on their knees (Acts 4:24–31). As the church grew, the apostles refused to become embroiled in administrative problems because of their resolute desire to model prayer in their leadership team (Acts 6:4). Through united prayer, they trusted God for miraculous divine interventions in times of extreme trouble (Acts 12:5–12). They received ministry direction through intense seasons of worshipful prayer (Acts 13:1–2).

> *Most of us were taught prayer is something we do almost exclusively on our own in a closet somewhere. In reality, early Christians learned to pray largely by praying together.*

What a contrast to our individualized culture. Most of us were taught prayer is something we do almost exclusively on our own in a closet somewhere. In reality, early Christians learned to pray largely by praying together.

Personally, I cannot imagine living a vibrant and balanced Christian life without a regular dose of both. Those who neglect the consistent habit of praying in extended fashion with a community of believers are robbing themselves of great blessing and balance. In a sense, they are trying to hop on one leg and finding the prayer journey difficult, at best.

Isolated by Individualism

"Why have we neglected the corporate emphasis on prayer found in . . . Acts and the epistles?" Gene Getz, noted professor from Dallas Theological Seminary, asks that question in his book *Praying for One Another,* and tells how we view biblical prayer from our bias rather than from the original intent and context of the Scriptures. He notes that our Western culture is distinguished by rugged individualism, and makes this observation:

> *We use the personal pronouns "I" and "my" and "me." We have not been taught to think in terms of "we" and "our" and "us." Consequently, we individualize many references to corporate experience in the New Testament, thus often emphasizing personal prayer. More is said in Acts and the Epistles about corporate prayer, corporate learning of biblical truth, corporate evangelism, and corporate Christian maturity and growth than about the personal aspects of these Christian disciplines. Don't misunderstand. Both are intricately related. But the personal dimensions of Christianity are difficult to maintain and practice consistently unless they grow out of a proper corporate experience on a regular basis.*[1]

In our Western culture, we have come to believe that it is more important to pray alone than with others. This is a symptom of our basic view of society. In his book *The Connecting Church,* Randy Frazee describes our culture of individualism. He explains that we are no longer born into a culture of community but a "way of life that makes the individual supreme or sovereign over everything."[2] Frazee documents this as a problem especially for those born after World War II. He laments the impact on the church by observing that we have "all too often mirrored the culture by making Christianity an individual sport."[3]

Group Instruction

We've looked at the Lord's Prayer as a model for the *content* of our praying. We should also embrace it as a model for the *context* of our prayers. Jesus said to His followers in Matthew 6:5, "And when you pray. . . ." He assumed they would gather in prayer as a regular part of their spiritual development. The pronoun here is plural, as Jesus is talking to them as a group about their engagement in prayer as a group. In our language, it would be "when you guys pray" or "when y'all pray" (in southern dialect). In other words, Jesus says, "When you all pray together as my followers, do it this way in your gatherings, not like those praise-hungry Pharisees or misguided Gentiles."

To support this idea, the pronouns are all plural in the pattern of prayer He gave. He did not give the instruction to pray, "*My* Father in heaven . . . give *me* this day *my* daily bread, and forgive *me my* debts . . . Do not lead *me* into temptation, but deliver *me* from the evil one . . ." Instead, this was a teaching passage on the mindset, motives, venue, and pattern of corporate praying in the lives of Jesus' followers.

Our Assumptions About Prayer

Today we read the commands about prayer in the New Testament epistles and assume they are primarily designed to motivate the individual believer in his or her private prayer time. We have come to believe that prayer is first and best experienced at a private level. For some of the zealots, it might be that they enjoy prayer in concert with others. Yet early Christians had a very different perspective.

We must keep in mind that until the advent of the printing

press, almost all learning was verbal and in community settings. This clearly affected the way believers received and applied the truth. Today, with individual copies of the Bible, we make the applications first, privately—then corporately, if at all.

> *Until the advent of the printing press, almost all learning was verbal and in community settings. This clearly affected the way believers received and applied the truth.*

In New Testament times, a letter would arrive from Paul, and believers had but one choice in order to receive this truth: They had to show up. *Period.* And when a command was read in the original language, the plural pronouns popped. The application to believers as a community was clear. As a result, they prayed together often, passionately and obediently.

Michael Griffiths reiterates this consideration when he writes, "In standard English, the second person singular 'you' and the second person plural 'you' are identical. Thus, New Testament Letters addressed to congregations are read (by us) as though they were addressed to the individuals. It is good and right that we should apply the Scriptures to ourselves personally, but it is unfortunate if we also apply the Scriptures individualistically and ignore the fact that the original intention was to instruct us not so much as individuals, but as whole communities of Christian people."[4]

Expanding the Closet

One very unfortunate cultural revision of the text involves the idea of the "closet." When Jesus said, "When thou prayest, enter into thy closet" (Matthew 6:6 KJV), just what did He mean? We usually assume a closet to be a small cubicle designed for our shoes, clothes, and possibly a flashlight.

This word, *tamion*, appears in the Greek New Testament four times. Among those instances it can mean "inner rooms" (Luke 12:3 NASB) or a "storehouse" or "storeroom" (Luke 12:24 KJV, NASB, NIV). The *New International Version, New American Standard*

Bible, and *New King James Version* all use a clearer idea when they describe this place of group prayer as a *room* or *inner room.* The narrow interpretation of a private chamber for solitary prayer is not a necessary or reasonable meaning. This would be especially difficult when Jesus spoke to a group of disciples, using plural pronouns. It would either have to be a very crowded private closet crammed with sweaty, cramping disciples—or it must mean a place large enough for a corporate gathering.

I have discovered that in 1611, when the King James Bible was translated, one of the primary usages of the word *closet* was the idea of a private meeting room, which makes perfect sense as to the selection of the word for that particular translation.[5]

The historical application of this principle is seen in Acts 1:12–2:1, where the disciples are gathered in an upper room, enjoying extended group prayer out of the public eye. This pattern continued in Acts as they responded to persecution (Acts 4:23–31), engaged in intercession for an imprisoned leader (12:12–17), and sought the Lord's direction for ministry (13:1–3). They advanced collectively on their knees.

Many believers struggle in learning how to pray. Hundreds of volumes have been written over the centuries on the theology and practice of prayer. Yet the most fundamental principle has often been neglected. Young Christians must learn to pray in community with mature believers. Prayer is vital for transformation, and corporate prayer is indispensable as a part of the process.

If I Were the Devil

Each week I write a devotional, which is distributed via e-mail to those who have signed up to receive it.[6] Recently my son, who works for our ministry, coordinating my schedule, has put these devotionals into book form.[7] One recent devotion was titled "If I Were the Devil." (My wife commented that some days she thinks I am!)

I noted that while the devil is NOT all-knowing, he is brilliant, supernatural, and shrewd from thousands of years of experience. He certainly knows some things. He knows the

Bible (James 2:19–20), so he knows the divine game plan for his defeat—and the vital role of prayer.

He knows church history. He is fully aware that his greatest defeats have come during seasons of spiritual awakening and revival, and that every one of these seasons of exponential spiritual transformation has been rooted in movements of united, biblical prayer.

He also knows human nature. He observes our tendency to live independently of God's supernatural provision for our lives. He was active in Laodicea, for example, as he assisted that church in living by their own riches, efforts, and sufficiency rather than pursuing intimacy with their Savior. He likes things this way.

Therefore, if I were the devil, I would use my best deceptive tools to keep Christians from praying in transforming ways—and especially to keep them from praying together. I would keep them busy and isolated from one another. I would do everything possible to keep them distracted and disinterested in biblical, balanced, revival-style prayer gatherings.

To accomplish this, I would do the following:

Fuel the spirit of rugged individualism. By keeping Christians independent of each other, I would keep them independent from God. I would keep them frustrated in their personal prayer lives by preventing them from learning to pray by praying together.

Dig ruts of boring prayer. When they did try to pray together, I would make sure the prayer meetings were based more on human needs than on God's power. I would do everything possible to encourage boredom and gossip in these gatherings so that most people would stay away from these passionless "prayer" times.

Delight in theological orthodoxy without spiritual passion. I would know how effective it is to get Bible-loving Christians to delight in theological correctness without spiritual intimacy. It worked very well in Ephesus (see Revelation 2:1–7), a once-great church that fell out of love with Jesus, even though they had great theology and teaching. I would let them be content with good sermons and grand theological ideas, as long as they stayed off their knees in trying to make it real in their hearts.

Encourage idle preaching on prayer. I would know that sermons on prayer frequently fall on deaf ears, especially when the leaders do not model prayer. I would keep pastors content with talking about inspiring prayer ideas as long as they did not actually lead their people into extraordinary gatherings of prayer. I would know that prayer information without prayer action anesthetizes Christians from spiritual reality.

Promote "success" in the ministry. Crazy as it sounds, I might even promote church growth as a replacement for real revival. I would encourage an interest in numbers, activities, strategies, and events. This would keep them away from brokenness, repentance, and passion for God's transforming presence. This would distract them from a real pursuit of the awakenings that have undermined my nefarious efforts.

Knowing that I could not keep people from eternal life because of the power of the gospel, I would at least try to keep them from eternal reward by getting them to rely on their own flesh rather than on the Spirit of God in their ministry efforts.

Yes, if I were the devil, this strategy would be one of my most important. I would amass all of my most subtle and deceptive troops and tools to prevent transforming prayer and spiritual awakening at all costs. As long as Christians were sincere but isolated, active but powerless, entertained but shallow, I would win.

Jesus' Plan: United in Transformation

In spite of the devil's malevolent intentions, the Lord Jesus has a triumphant, supernatural plan and we must embrace it with resolve. In Mark 11:17, Jesus made His intentions clear: "Then He taught, saying to them, 'Is it not written, "My house shall be called a house of prayer for all nations"? But you have made it a "den of thieves." ' " Jesus knew the kind of power He was able to unleash in humble, dependent people who would allow Him to bear the fruit of His life and power through prayer. Again, that is why He started the church with His people on their knees. He sustained and blessed the church the same way.

> *In spite of the devil's malevolent intentions, the Lord Jesus has a triumphant, supernatural plan and we must embrace it with resolve.*

Still today, He wants His church to be characterized by an environment of life-giving prayer.

Paul, when instructing Timothy in how to establish church function and order in his first letter to his young disciple, made the priority of prayer very clear again. He wrote, "Therefore I exhort *first of all* that supplications, prayers, intercessions, and giving of thanks be made for all men" (1 Timothy 2:1). Prayer was not supposed to be the only thing the church did, just the first thing they did. That's the way Jesus wanted it to be.

The "Why" Behind the "Where"

We have seen that a vital part of transformational prayer is the priority of praying in community. In doing so, we learn to pray more effectively (assuming these prayer meetings are transformational in design). We enjoy a greater consistency and accountability.

We have seen that our culture of rugged individualism gravitates against this biblical understanding and that our understanding of the "closet" may have fueled our excuses in not gathering with greater passion. We have observed that the enemy of our souls is likely working to keep us away from powerful experiences of prayer. Yet Jesus has made it clear that He desires us to be a "house of prayer."

Ultimately, however, we come full circle—back to the glory of God. I want to refer again to Paul's comments on the goal of the church gathering in prayer. He wrote, "While you also cooperate by your prayers for us [helping and laboring together with us]. Thus [the lips of] many persons [turned toward God will eventually] give thanks on our behalf for the grace (the blessing of deliverance) granted us at the request of the many who have prayed" (2 Corinthians 1:11 AMP).

Paul reminds us that when we pray together and bear

collective witness to His answers to prayer, God receives greater thanksgiving. God is glorified in our thanksgiving. Our thanksgiving is greater because we have prayed together.

When we pray together in a worship-based fashion, not only is God glorified in our very act of collective adoration but also in our ongoing recognition of His transforming power, both in and through us as He advances His gospel and glory in this world. (For detailed information about how to organize a local church prayer summit, visit *www.transformingprayerbook.com*.)

> *When we pray together and bear collective witness to His answers to prayer, God receives greater thanksgiving.*

I Am Now Entirely Free:
A Trophy of Transformation

by SANDI S.—HOMEMAKER,
CALIFORNIA

For sixteen years I have practiced this thing called worship-based prayer both corporately and privately. In that time, I have learned to recognize the voice of God and know when He is speaking to me. Many times I have experienced the felt presence of God when He "shows up" among His people as they pray together. I have seen the Lord heal the sick, give meaning to the lives of Christians who are depressed or suicidal, and fire up the passion for Him that has become cold for many believers, returning life to their eyes and joy to their hearts. I have even seen people get saved who thought they were Christians because they went to church, prayed, and served God their whole lives but had never yielded their will to His and asked for forgiveness.

The effect this kind of praying has had on me is a faith in God so rich and deep that the trials I have faced—extended unemployment, financial hardship, foreclosure, demonic attacks, miscarriage, high-risk pregnancy, and years with chronic pain—have not shaken it. It has made my marriage strong and filled with love, kept our family unit knitted together, and brought an inexplicable joy to my soul.

Many people have said to me, "I pray in my head all day long. Isn't that good enough?" No. Presenting a list of "I want this" and "Give me that" without first spending time thanking Jesus—who has sacrificed so much for us—without praising Him, honoring Him, and confessing our sins to Him, is like spitting arrogance into the face of God. That kind of praying is selfish and nets little, if any, results. To those people I would say, if you listen to Jesus' teaching on the subject of prayer and then do it His way, you will experience God like you have never experienced Him before, and you will never want to go back to your old way of praying again!

CHAPTER 17

Your Role in Organic Revival

If Jesus answered all of your prayers from the last thirty days,
would anything change in THE world or just YOUR world?

JOHN W. BRYSON

Revive us, and we will call upon Your name.
Restore us, O Lord God of hosts;
Cause Your face to shine,
And we shall be saved!

PSALM 80:18–19

Imagine waking up one morning to discover these front-page headlines in papers across the nation:

- *Detroit News*: Three Islamic Mullahs and Dozens of Other Muslim Leaders Join Christian Churches
- *Washington Post*: Five Jewish Priests Leave Synagogue to Follow Jesus After Dramatic Conversion
- *Seattle Times*: Surveys Show Bible Sales Up 200% in Recent Weeks
- *San Francisco Chronicle*: Bill Maher Apologizes to Christians After Becoming Born Again
- *Miami Herald*: Adult Book Stores Closing Across Region After Dramatic Downturn in Sales

- *Denver Post*: Churches in Area Boom With Record Attendance; Religious Leaders Cannot Explain Why

Could these things really happen? Is the transforming power of Jesus Christ still able to accomplish such exploits? Does it stir your heart to dream of being a part of this kind of movement of God's Spirit?

Something very much like these headlines appears in the New Testament, in one of my favorite "revival" passages. In the first five chapters of Acts, the people were being "added" to the church daily. By Acts 6:1, the number of the disciples was "multiplying." Some estimate that the church could have reached as many as twenty thousand men and women at this point.[1] No doubt the church was alive by the power of Christ.

However, just six verses later we read this account of a re-enlivened church: "Then the word of God spread, and the number of the disciples *multiplied greatly* in Jerusalem, and a great many of the priests were obedient to the faith" (Acts 6:7).

Imagine this. The disciples are already growing beyond number. Now they are "multiplying greatly." Try to count that! In addition, the "word of God spread" in some profound way, even beyond the previous impact. Now a "great many of the priests" are becoming obedient to the faith. *Incredible.* These hard-line opponents of the gospel had conspired to crucify Christ. They had been persecuting the church. Now a great number of them are converting to Christianity. What an amazing resurgence of the power of God through His people.

What Sparks Revival?

If you examine Acts 6 to see what sparked this amazing movement of the Spirit, you will not find three quick steps to church growth. In fact, you will learn that this situation was birthed from a major problem in the inadvertent neglect of some of the widows in the daily food distribution program. The potential of division and distraction loomed.

The solution rested in two important decisions. First, the leaders resolved not to jump in and design a new program.

Instead they said, "We will give ourselves continually to prayer and to the ministry of the word" (Act 6:4). Second, they had an authentic confidence in the sufficiency of Spirit in the people to resolve the problem through the selection of a godly team of coordinators. God blessed their faith and unleashed a whole new wave of spiritual power that advanced the gospel in exponential fashion.

I believe these apostles knew, first and foremost, that they needed to maintain the environment of spiritual power that had proven to be the secret to God's blessing. This was an environment of extraordinary prayer and bold adherence to the Word. They knew if this environment was to grow, they had to lead it by their own example. They dedicated great amounts of their time to praying together and leading the church in seeking the Lord.

Sadly, today we have a different scenario in most churches. Leaders have become program designers, savvy administrators, and problem solvers. The people generally sit, soak, and sour as they watch the professionals run the show. The power we see in Acts 6:1–7 captures a different picture.

We need an Acts 6 revival. Revival is not a week of evangelistic meetings or a televised healing crusade. It is a period of unusual blessing when God brings a supernatural re-enlivening to His people. Dr. A. T. Pierson, pastor and missionary leader from the 1800s, observed: "There has never been a spiritual awakening in any country or locality that did not begin in united prayer."[2] It is broadly believed that whenever God wanted to bring a great work of revival, He always began by sending His people to their knees. We see this principle in 2 Chronicles 7:14 ("If my people . . . will humble themselves, and pray and seek My face . . ."), and we see it demonstrated in a fresh wave of power here in Acts 6:1–7.

> *Revival is not a week of evangelistic meetings or a televised healing crusade. It is a period of unusual blessing when God brings a supernatural re-enlivening to His people.*

History has proven the power of great revivals to awaken God's people from spiritual slumber and to call them to humility, repentance, and a fresh desperation for Christ's presence and power. As a result, the church has become a channel of the supernatural power of Christ to awaken a society with the power of the gospel. Typically, an unprecedented evangelistic advancement occurred and many practical blessings unfolded in the culture because of the positive impact of the gospel. If you've never done so, I would encourage you to read some of the amazing accounts of the awakenings that shook our nation and the world in centuries past.[3]

Jumping Off the Cliff

In 2007, I became so captivated by the need for revival and my desire to play some small role in mobilizing the kind of prayer that could move us in that direction, I did something crazy. I left the security and prominence of leading a large church and became a support-raising missionary. I essentially jumped off the cliff without a parachute in order to have the freedom to speak, write, lead prayer events, and somehow help encourage a much-needed awakening. I went from being a senior pastor to a full-time "spiritual pyromaniac." Of course, I did this in perfect sequence with the worst economy in seventy years. Still, God has been faithful, and the ministry has been fruitful.

Why would anyone do something so crazy? My heart is driven by a vision. *Vision* has been described as a picture of what *could be* coupled with the conviction that it *must be*. So, IF Christ began to move in such a way that believers around the nation, continent, and world began to humble themselves and pray and seek His face, and turn from their wicked ways—what might it look like for God to hear from heaven, forgive our sins, and heal our land? This is our ultimate BHAG (Big Holy Audacious Goal). Could we dream together that Christ could awaken our society in our lifetime?

Ultimately, the goal is not only that you experience transformation or that your circle of friends feels the change or even that your church becomes spiritually reawakened. If these realities are authentic, it will spill into the community and beyond in powerful, Christ-exalting fashion.

Can We Organize an Awakening?

These days, it seems everyone is trying to drum up excitement for another revival event or program. There is no shortage of ideas afloat about how we all need to converge at some big gathering to get a transforming touch among the masses that have traveled far and wide to find a new angle on prayer and renewal. Some of these gatherings are designed to call down God's fire; others focus on the need to wait quietly on some new revelation. I am sure the organizers are sincere and certainly dedicated. Each has some biblical guidelines that motivate all the activity. Certainly God can use these events for His glory.

Yet all are expensive and complicated to organize. The promotional machinery involved in making these events occur is nothing less that gargantuan. The dollars flow like water as the "lights, cameras, and action" are all prepared for the big day when God will show up. In some cases celebrity Christians are key to attracting a crowd. I suppose participants might walk away wondering who really got the credit for the big event—and who kept the leftover cash. It feels like we are expected to finance someone else's visionary grandiosity.

In the rush of getting God to show up at another revival event, I wonder if we might not need to slow down, tone down, and get down to the humble, quiet, grassroots spiritual transformation that revivals are made of in intimacy and obscurity.

Honestly, I find myself wondering if this is really the Lord's best plan for reviving His church. In the rush of getting God to show up at another revival event, I wonder if we might not need to slow down, tone down, and get down to the humble, quiet, grassroots spiritual transformation that revivals are made of in intimacy and obscurity.

Dreaming Organic

I am dreaming of something more organic. I hope you will too. *Organic* refers to something "arising as a natural outgrowth." The vision for organic revival that moves my heart today looks like this: "Pastor-led, local church-oriented movements of Christ-exalting, worship-based prayer—leading to a full-scale revival, supernatural evangelism, and cultural transformation." My friends call it my hyper-hyphenated vision. Put more simply, it is to see the next Great Awakening in our generation.

Essentially, this is what drives my desire to equip individuals and pastors to experience transforming prayer in the context of life. It is the longing to see churches become houses of prayer, distinguished by spiritual passion and endurance. The goal is clearly not the elevation of any church, ministry, or personality, but that Christ would receive glory as congregations around the nation awaken to His presence and purposes. It is worship-based prayer that cultivates a deep repentance in His presence, a growing desperation for His power, and an unquenchable passion for His renown.

> *It is worship-based prayer that cultivates a deep repentance in His presence, a growing desperation for His power, and an unquenchable passion for His renown.*

I believe as pastors embrace an extraordinary commitment to prayer and His Word (Acts 6:4), and believers engage in experiences of transforming prayer, a full-scale revival could occur in the environment of praying churches. The water-level of awakening would rise. Congregations in the North, South, East, and West—large and small, and of various denominational stripes—would experience His glory. Out of this movement, profound evangelism would occur, as it historically occurred in previous revivals. Ultimately, our culture would be transformed by the gospel as manifested through a glorious church. Then the tide would turn.[4]

Change Starts Now

You can be a vital part of this compelling and essential vision. Ultimately, this kind of revival starts with my heart, my home, my church, and my community. If you pray that for me—and I pray that for you—and we act in faith to seek His face, something organic and glorious might just occur. It is worth dreaming about, worth seeking after, and worth living for.

My friend Byron Paulus says, "The biggest billboard for revival is a changed life." That is the beautiful outcome of transforming prayer. Thanks for joining me in the journey. May God be magnified!

APPENDIX 1

The Privileges, Possibilities, and Provision Related to Prayer

I have heard it said that nothing is dynamic until it is specific. To say that the power and potential of prayer is dynamic is an understatement tantamount to saying the sun is bright and hot. Yet specificity fuels deeper appreciation. Counting the many blessings and benefits of prayer can ignite fresh vision and passion for what Christ can do in us, for us, and through us when we seriously embrace prayer. Let's take a moment to consider the privileges, explore the possibilities, and imagine the provision available to us because of God's gift of prayer to our hearts.

Prayer Has Its Privileges

Consider the privileges available to us in prayer:

- In prayer, we experience the most intimate and powerful spiritual exercise known to humanity (Psalm 131; Romans 8:14; Galatians 4:6).
- In prayer, we talk freely about our secret struggles, frustrated feelings, and our murky motives with words that are raw and unfiltered—yet understood by an all-knowing, all-powerful God (Psalm 62:8; Hebrews 4:16).

- In prayer, we find protection when we are vulnerable and experience security when we are unsure (Psalm 34:4; 56:3; 2 Corinthians 1:8–11).

- In prayer, we accept our weaknesses, surrender our rights, and ask for help from the only One who can create permanent change (2 Chronicles 20:12; Psalm 40:17; Luke 22:42; 2 Corinthians 12:8–10).

- In prayer, we abide through intimate connection to the life-giving power of the risen Christ (John 15:4–5; Ephesians 3:16–19; Colossians 1:9–10).

- In prayer, we trade in our anxieties for the peace that passes all understanding (Psalm 29:11; Isaiah 26:3; Philippians 4:6–7).

- In prayer, we receive wisdom for the perplexities and doubts we face (2 Chronicles 1:10; Proverbs 2:3–6; James 1:5).

- In prayer, we cast our burdens on the One who has the power to work all things out for our good and His glory (Psalm 55:22; Romans 8:26–28; 1 Peter 5:7).

- In prayer, desperate and lost people receive mercy and grace that saves and transforms (Luke 18:13; Romans 10:13).

- In prayer, faith grows and God's people arise to call on Him boldly for miraculous exploits from His hand (Jeremiah 33:3; Mark 9:23–24; 11:23–24; Acts 12:5–8).

- In prayer, we receive grace to become like Christ, even when the problems persist and the burdens remain (2 Corinthians 3:18; 12:9–10).

- In prayer, we find the power and perseverance to defeat Satan and overcome his schemes (Luke 22:32; Ephesians 6:18; James 4:7).

- In prayer, we discover the beauty and power of intimacy and satisfaction in God (Psalm 27:4, 8; 73:25–26).

Explore the Possibilities

Consider the possibilities available through prayer:

- In prayer, believers discover a level of trust and unity of heart that is truly supernatural, given our many differences in perspective and personality (Acts 1:14; 13:1–2).
- In prayer, families receive grace, health, and persevering love to sacrifice and stay together (Psalm 127; Acts 16:31–34).
- In prayer, God prompts, prepares, and propels Christians to become actively engaged in His evangelistic mission in this world (Matthew 9:38; Acts 4:31; 13:1–3).
- In prayer, leaders receive supernatural insight into the truth of God's Word and wisdom for shepherding His people (Acts 6:2–4; Acts 13:1–2).
- In prayer, major revivals have been birthed, leading to dramatic and lasting transformation of lives, churches, communities, and nations (Acts 6:7).
- In prayer, we receive boldness, wisdom, and opportunities to share the truth of the gospel (Ephesians 6:18–20; Colossians 4:3–4).
- In prayer, God works powerfully to bring glory to himself, not through human efforts but through humble dependence (2 Chronicles 20:18–23; John 17; 2 Corinthians 1:10–11).

Provision in Abundance

Consider the provision God has made for us to pray:

- For prayer, Christ went to the cross, offering His life and blood, demonstrating the price that was paid for the privilege of prayer (Ephesians 2:18; Hebrews 10:12–14).
- For prayer, the temple veil was miraculously torn in two to demonstrate the availability of the presence and power of God through the finished work of Christ (Matthew 27:50–51; Hebrews 6:19–20; 10:19–22).

- For prayer, sinful hearts are cleansed and become permanent temples of His Spirit, who teaches and guides us to deeper intimacy and greater power (Romans 8:15–17; 26–27; 1 Corinthians 2:9–12).

- For prayer, Jesus now lives, making perpetual intercession for us before the Father, as our sympathetic high priest, that our prayers might be heard and answered (Romans 8:34; Hebrews 7:25; 1 John 2:1–2).

- For prayer, the very Holy of Holies is now open 24/7 with a welcome sign that says to every true believer, "Enter boldly!" (Hebrews 4:14–16; 10:19–22).

Face-to-Face Biblical Encounters with God

In both the Old and New Testaments, we find accounts of individuals blessed and changed by an encounter with God's face.

Old Testament

- Abraham encountered the presence of Almighty God and fell on his face in humble worship (Genesis 17:3). God's covenantal blessing and the promise of a son emerged from this encounter.

- Moses spoke to the Lord "face to face, as a man speaks to his friend." He taught Joshua to do the same (Exodus 33:11–12). The mark of their lives and leadership is that the Lord was with them (Joshua 1:17; 3:7). They sought His face and manifested His presence. Still, Moses experienced a unique intimacy. At the time of his death it was noted, "But since then there has not arisen in Israel a prophet like Moses, whom the Lord knew face to face" (Deuteronomy 34:10).

- Gideon's military exploits included a moment when he encountered the Angel of the Lord, receiving the assurance of peace and the promise of God's powerful presence.

In response he declares, "Alas, O Lord God! For I have seen the Angel of the Lord face to face" (Judges 6:22). Confidence and courage came when this leader encountered God.

- David wrote compellingly of his experience of seeking God's face. In Psalm 17:15, he said, "As for me, I will see Your face in righteousness; I shall be satisfied when I awake in Your likeness." He described true worshipers, walking in God's blessing, as "the generation of those who seek Him, who seek Your face" (Psalm 24:6). In Psalm 27:4, he resolved that his one desire was to experience God's presence and behold the beauty of the Lord. In the midst of persecution and perplexity, David wrote, "Make Your face shine upon Your servant; save me for Your mercies' sake" (Psalm 31:16). He knew that face-to-face intimacy was the secret to his integrity and his wisdom (Psalm 41:12; 119:135).

  When that intimacy was interrupted, David knew it. In Psalm 30:7, he wrote, "By Your favor You have made my mountain stand strong; You hid Your face, and I was troubled." Again, in Psalm 27:9, he prayed, "Do not hide Your face from me; do not turn Your servant away in anger; You have been my help; do not leave me nor forsake me, O God of my salvation." We see his great prayer of confession, where he recognized his violation of God's holy presence: "Hide Your face from my sins, and blot out all my iniquities" (Psalm 51:9). David was a man after God's own heart—and he understood what it meant to seek His face.

- Job—a man of great integrity, patience, and endurance— was tested severely by God in almost every category of his life. During his personal audience with Almighty God, Job learned the core lesson of his encounter. In response, Job prayed, "I have heard of You by the hearing of the ear, but now my eye sees You. Therefore I abhor myself, and repent in dust and ashes" (Job 42:5–6). Face to face, Job became aware of the deep issues of his heart, repented, and went to the next level in his intimacy with the Almighty. Blessings followed.

- Isaiah saw the Lord high and lifted up, surrounded by seraphim and radiant in His holiness (Isaiah 6:1–8). This face-to-face encounter drove him to cry out in confession, "Woe is me, for I am undone!" From that awesome moment of worship, confession, and cleansing, Isaiah received his call and responded, "Here am I! Send me." When we seek His face, we are cleansed, changed, and called into vital service for His kingdom.

New Testament

- Thomas saw the faith and hope of his colleagues after their gathering with the risen Christ. Thomas was not among them in their initial encounter. Days later, he "saw for himself" as Jesus again appeared. Addressing Thomas directly, the Lord told Thomas to reach out and touch His wounds, but all Thomas needed to do was see Jesus and he was transformed from doubt to bold declaration, proclaiming Jesus as his Lord and God (John 20:28).
- Paul was on a road trip hunting down the "people of the way" who were multiplying like rabbits and posing a threat to the Jewish religious system. At the instant he met the risen Lord face-to-face, he fell to the ground. In the days following, he was physically blind, but captivated with the face of Christ as he prayed on Straight Street (Acts 9:11). His hunger grew so much that he spent three years on the backside of a desert, seeking Christ and learning from Him. Face time turned Paul into the greatest missionary the world has ever known.
- John, the elderly apostle, was banished on the Isle of Patmos. As he worshiped on the Lord's Day, he encountered a powerful face-to-face moment with the risen Jesus. He described Christ's face with these words: "His head and hair were white like wool, as white as snow, and His eyes like a flame of fire. . . . His voice as the sound of many waters . . . and His countenance was like the sun shining in its strength" (Revelation 1:14–16). And what did John do? He writes, "And when I saw Him, I fell at His

feet as dead. But He laid His right hand on me, saying to me, 'Do not be afraid; I am the First and the Last. I am He who lives, and was dead, and behold, I am alive forevermore. Amen. And I have the keys of Hades and of Death' " (Revelation 1:17–18).

This is the Christ whose face we seek. How can we be content with anything less when we consider the privilege of prayer? How can we remain the same when we encounter the living God in authentic intimacy?

APPENDIX 3

How Jesus Prayed

- Matthew 11:25—He thanked the Father for His pleasure in hiding truth from some and revealing it to others.
- John 11:41–42—Jesus publicly thanks the Father that He hears His prayers so that others will believe the Father sent Him.
- John 12:27–28—Jesus openly acknowledges His troubled soul in light of His impending sacrifice on the cross, but affirms His commitment to the purpose of His coming to earth, declaring, "Father, glorify Your name."
- John 17—In His high priestly prayer, Jesus reflects on the finished task of bringing glory to the Father through His earthly ministry, while asking for the spiritual preservation and unity of His followers for the sake of convincing the unbelieving world that the Father has sent the Son.
- Luke 22:31–32—Jesus prays for Peter that his faith will not fail "as Satan sifts him like wheat" so that in time Peter will return to Christ and strengthen the faith of others.
- Matthew 26:39, 42; Mark 14:36; Luke 22:42—Jesus prays to the Father, desiring that the "cup of suffering" pass from Him, but declaring, "Not as I will, but as You will."

- While suffering on the cross, Jesus prays to the Father three times. First, "Father, forgive them, for they do not know what they do" (Luke 23:34), an amazing prayer of mercy and grace. Second, "My God, My God, why have You forsaken Me?" (Matthew 27:46; Mark 15:34), revealing the weight of the condemnation of sin that Jesus bore on our behalf. Third, "Father, into Your hands I commit My spirit" (Luke 23:46), in which Jesus willingly offers himself in death, as He completes the atoning work.

APPENDIX 4

Paul's Prayer Requests

In 2 Corinthians 1:9–11, we see that the Corinthians had been praying for Paul as he faced death in Asia Minor. We do not know exactly what they prayed, but we do know that Paul was delivered from this life-threatening trial and from self-reliance. The result was a greater faith in Christ and united thanksgiving to God.

In Romans 15:30–33, Paul asks the believers in Rome to strive together with him in prayer because of their regard for Christ and the Spirit's love in their hearts. He specifically requests prayer for protection from the enemies of the gospel, blessing in the delivery of his love offering to the suffering church in Jerusalem, and God's will in bringing him joyfully to Rome, where he hopes to find refreshing rest in their company.

In considering Paul's desire for deliverance, it is insightful to think about his conversation with the Ephesian elders, which occurred while he was on this very journey to Jerusalem, then to Rome. He told them in Acts 20:23–24, "The Holy Spirit testifies in every city, saying that chains and tribulations await me. But none of these things move me; nor do I count my life dear to myself, so that I may finish my race with joy, and the ministry which I received from the Lord Jesus, to testify to the gospel of the grace of God." It seems his sole desire for deliverance and survival was for the singular purpose of the gospel, not his own comfort or avoidance of suffering.

In Ephesians 6:19, Paul adds a personal postscript to his great teaching on spiritual warfare by asking for prayer. He asks them to pray "that utterance may be given to me, that I may open my mouth boldly to make known the mystery of the gospel." He wrote this from prison, but made no mention of a painful trial or his need for a vacation.

In Philippians 1:19, Paul writes again from prison. He asks that they would pray that the Spirit of Jesus Christ would provide his deliverance. Yet in the context, he is content with either deliverance *to* death and his eternal reward—or a deliverance *from* death and the continuation of his responsibilities of serving others through the gospel. He wrote clearly about his motive for receiving these prayers when he spoke of his ultimate desire that "Christ will be magnified in my body, whether by life or by death" (Philippians 1:20).

Still writing from prison, Paul asks the fellow believers in Colossae to pray for him, "that God would open to us a door for the word, to speak the mystery of Christ, for which I am also in chains, that I may make it manifest, as I ought to speak" (Colossians 4:3–4). The passionate apostle seemed unconcerned about comfort or survival. He just wanted to fulfill the gospel purpose of his life.

Paul, in his first letter to the Thessalonians, simply writes, "Brethren, pray for us," without including any requests. In his second letter to the Thessalonians, he again requests prayer, asking for deliverance from unreasonable and wicked men so "that the word of the Lord may run swiftly and be glorified" (2 Thessalonians 3:1).

APPENDIX 5

The Bible and God's Glory

It is clear from Scripture that Christ saves us for God's glory and sets us apart to himself for His glory.

Writing about "our Lord Jesus Christ, who gave Himself for our sins, that He might deliver us from this present evil age, according to the will of our God and Father," Paul exclaims, "to whom be *glory* forever and ever. Amen" (Galatians 1:3–5). To the Ephesians, Paul speaks of our God's amazing grace in Christ through our election, adoption, and forgiveness—"to the praise of the *glory* of His grace" (Ephesians 1:6), "to the praise of His *glory*" (v. 12), and again, "to the praise of His *glory*" (v. 14).

Second Corinthians 5:15 exclaims that "He died for all, that those who live should live no longer for themselves, but for Him who died for them and rose again." Because we were "bought at a price" we are compelled to *"glorify* God in [our] body and in [our] spirit, which are God's" (1 Corinthians 6:20).

The elderly apostle John declared, "To Him who loved us and washed us from our sins in His own blood, and has made us kings and priests to His God and Father, to Him be *glory* and dominion forever and ever. Amen" (Revelation 1:5–6).

The same atoning sacrifice God provided through His Son to save us also made a way for us to enter the Holy of Holies. Calvary's power tore the veil that separated sinful man from a

Holy God and made possible an intimate experience with Him. Now, in light of the price He paid, we must pray for the goal of His glory—embracing the full purpose of our salvation.

Set Apart for His Glory

As believers, we now have the assurance that God is working in us "both to will and to do for His good pleasure" (Philippians 2:13). We are being set apart to God and made more like Jesus. Why? For His glory.

We grow as we embrace "all the promises of God" that are *Yes* and *Amen* in Christ—"to the *glory* of God through us" (2 Corinthians 1:20). We are "being filled with the fruits of righteousness which are by Jesus Christ, to the *glory* and praise of God" (Philippians 1:11). As we comprehend His love and power in us, it will result in His "*glory* in the church by Christ Jesus to all generations, forever and ever" (Ephesians 3:21).

The apostle Peter reminds us that our faith is sometimes tested by fire so that our lives "may be found to praise, honor, and *glory* at the revelation of Jesus Christ" (1 Peter 1:7). He reminds us to serve in the power God provides "that in all things God may be *glorified* through Jesus Christ, to whom belong the *glory* and the dominion forever and ever" (1 Peter 4:11). He concludes his letter with the assurance that "the God of all grace, who called us to His eternal *glory* by Christ Jesus, after you have suffered a while, perfect, establish, strengthen, and settle you" for the ultimate goal: "To Him be the *glory* and the dominion forever and ever. Amen" (1 Peter 5:10–11). Peter also concludes his second letter, reminding us of our calling to "grow in the grace and knowledge of our Lord and Savior Jesus Christ" with the result: "To Him be the *glory* both now and forever" (2 Peter 3:18).

Jude, the half-brother of Jesus, reassures us with these words: "Now to Him who is able to keep you from stumbling, and to present you faultless before the presence of His *glory* with exceeding joy, to God our Savior, who alone is wise, be *glory* and majesty, dominion and power, both now and forever. Amen" (Jude 24–25). He sets us apart and keeps us in His grace—for His glory.

Chapter-by-Chapter Questions for Application and Discussion

These questions are designed for group discussion but can also be used to help you in personal reflection and application.

Introduction: The Road to Real Change

1. We've considered the idea that prayer changes us. Can you think of a prayer experience in your life where you sensed that you were changed in a powerful way? Describe the experience and the change. In what way do you long for more of this kind of transformation? Pray that God would use the truths of this book to accomplish that work in your life.

2. Do you know other Christians whose lives have been transformed because of the reality of prayer? Have you ever asked them about their journey? If so, what did you discover? If no, seek them out and see what you can learn.

3. Many Christians today have become complacent about prayer. They do not see it as a transforming experience. Why do you think this happens for some believers? What do you think needs to happen in their lives to reawaken them to the power of prayer? Ask the Lord to do this work in your circles of friends and in your church.

Chapter 1: Beyond a "Grocery List" of Needs

1. D. A Carson notes, "Christians learn to pray by listening to those around them." How have you learned to pray in your spiritual journey? Who have most influenced you in a positive fashion? What lessons did they teach you? Take time to thank them for their influence.

2. What negative patterns have you learned in your efforts to pray? How have these patterns limited your growth? What can you do to embrace more biblical ideas in your prayer life?

3. Review the explanation of worship-based prayer. What aspects of this approach seem to be most intriguing to you? How might this approach encourage a greater level of personal transformation in your life?

Chapter 2: The Potential for Transformation

1. Review the list of privileges we enjoy through prayer in the associated appendix 2. Select four or five of these specific ideas and take time to thank the Lord for how you have seen them realized in your life.

2. Reflect on the truth offered by Jim Cymbala that "we will not one day stand before Christ to announce the *size* of our ministry, but to give an account of the *substance* of our ministry." Compare this idea with 1 Corinthians 3:9–15. What in your life today reflects the "wood, hay, and stubble" of a prayer-deficient life? How would you like to see your life changed to the "gold, silver, and precious stones" that spring from a Christ-centered life?

3. Review the five fruits of transforming prayer listed in this chapter. Which two would you most like to see reflected in your life in the coming months? Why?

Chapter 3: What Is Blocking the Breakthrough?

1. In this chapter you will find six realities that can hinder effective prayer. Which one of these represents a primary barrier you have experienced? Confess this to

the Lord in prayer and ask Him to give you the grace to move beyond this barrier to a greater experience of transformation.

2. We need to find prayer models from whom we can learn to pray more effectively. Ask the Lord to bring to mind an individual or group that might challenge you in your prayer life. Make it a goal to join that prayer experience and keep a journal on the lessons you learn.

3. Throughout this book, you will find testimonies of people whose lives were radically changed by spending extended time with the Lord in prayer, sometimes several days. Have you done this before? When will you find time to pursue this experience? If you do this, what do you think you might learn?

Chapter 4: Face Time!

1. After reading about seeking God's face, think of a time in your life when this was a reality for you. What made your prayer time so extraordinary? How did it impact your life? Thank the Lord for this experience and commit your heart to seeking His face on a regular basis.

2. In this chapter and in appendix 2, you will find a variety of biblical examples of individuals who sought God's face. Which one stands out to you as a challenge to your own heart? Why does this example stir you? What can you do to follow that example today?

3. Review the truths found in the Aaronic blessing (Numbers 6:24–26). What does this tell you about God's desire to reveal himself to His people? What blessings will occur in our lives as a result?

Chapter 5: Glowin' Moses and a Transformed You

1. What did you learn in this chapter about the concept of glory? How did the definitions and descriptions speak to your heart? How would you like to see greater glory in your life and church?

2. Review 2 Corinthians 3:17–4:1. In what way does this passage seem essential to how we understand prayer? How are the ideas here crucial to Christian ministry? What can you do to engage more fully in these spiritual realities in order to be more effective for Christ?

3. Now review 2 Corinthians 4:2–7. List the ministry results you find here, flowing from the transformation described in 2 Corinthians 3:18. How would you like your own impact on others to reflect these truths? Ask God to transform your life through prayer—and to transform the way you pray in order to experience this kind of influence.

Chapter 6: The Case of the Missing Prayer List

1. Have you ever offered the Lord "prayer leftovers," as described in this chapter? Think about what that looked like. Why do you think this can easily happen in our prayer lives? What can we do to avoid it?

2. Review the characteristics of "acceptable sacrifices" listed in this chapter. Which of these ideals challenge your heart today about the presentation of your heart and life to Christ? Ask the Lord for grace to live a life of acceptable sacrifice for His honor.

3. As you consider the traditional use of prayer lists, what do you think are some of the positive benefits of a list? What are the potential dangers? What changes, if any, do you plan to make in how you use prayer lists?

Chapter 7: All Prayer Requests Are Not Created Equal

1. As you think about the needs the Lord would have you pray about, do you sense a need for greater spiritual spontaneity, as described by A. W. Tozer? In what ways could you be more sensitive to the leadership of the Holy Spirit in prayer today?

2. Review the section about the pattern of Jesus' prayer life in appendix 3. Is there application here for your own prayers? How could you pray more like Jesus this week?

3. Reconsider the examples from the prayer life of the apostle Paul. In your own words, how would you summarize the heart and focus of his prayers and prayer requests? Is there something you could adjust in your prayers to better align with the biblical example of Paul?

Chapter 8: Go for the Glory!

1. This chapter challenges us to be motivated in our praying by a desire for God's glory, yet so often our motives contradict that goal. Make a list of desires that have motivated your prayers in the past (good ones and not so good). Surrender each of these to the Lord, asking Him for the grace to aim more passionately for His glory.

2. Describe one of the requests on your heart today. Consider the possible outcomes of this situation. Pray about how God could be glorified in these outcomes. Take the time to pray with the intention of seeking God's glory above all else.

3. Review Paul's longings expressed in Philippians 1:19–26. What ultimate aspiration did he embrace in life and in death? Think of someone you know who is faced with many opportunities. Pray for that person to focus on God's glory in all they do. Think of someone you know who is struggling with health issues or even facing death. Pray for God's glory to be revealed in that person's life and to all those involved in that life as well.

Chapter 9: How Abiding Guides Our Asking

1. Think of the times when your prayers began without the Scriptures to guide you. Did your prayers seem effective? What were the results? Did you have trouble keeping your mind from being distracted? If so, why?

2. Read through one of your favorite psalms, noting the truths you find about God's character. Now take time to simply praise God for His acts and attributes, without

asking for anything. Did you find this way of praying helped to focus your mind and heart?

3. Make a list of some of the positive benefits of basing your prayers in the Scriptures. Then ask the Lord to make these benefits real in your life as you continue to allow His Word to influence you as you pray.

Chapter 10: How His Spirit Ignites Our Supplication

1. Think again of the illustration of the Holy Spirit as a 24/7, indwelling prayer tutor. Now consider the credibility and skill of your tutor as described in John 16:13–14. List a few ways your prayer life could grow with the help of the Holy Spirit. Praise God for these truths as you pray today.

2. Read again the story of Jen Barrick. How does her story inspire you to trust the work of the Holy Spirit in your life, even when you feel limited in your understanding of prayer and the ways of God? How can you more consciously yield to the Holy Spirit as you pray today?

3. Even if you prayed from the Scripture, but did not rely on the wisdom and guidance of the Holy Spirit, how would you be missing the goal of prayer? Read 1 Corinthians 2:9–12. How does the Holy Spirit help us go beyond a merely intellectual approach to the Bible and prayer?

Chapter 11: How His Name Corrects Our Nonsense

1. We've seen that praying in Jesus' name is more than tacking those three words at the end of a prayer. Can you think of times when you prayed in Jesus' name for some crazy things? List or describe a few of them. After reading this chapter, how would you approach those requests differently?

2. Look at the list of Jesus' I AM statements. Then engage in a responsive prayer exercise. Use these statements in your prayer, e.g., "Lord Jesus, because you are _____ (an I AM description) my prayers will be _____ (describe the new way you will pray)."

3. Review John 14:10–14; 15:16–17; and 16:23–24. List the blessings that we experience when we pray in Jesus' name. Which of these represents a deep longing of your heart? With this desire in mind, ask the Lord to teach you how to pray more effectively in Jesus' name.

Chapter 12: How Revelation Motivates Our Response

1. Read Romans 11:33–12:2. Here is an example of "revelation and response." What truths do you find about God's character in this passage? What kind of response does the apostle Paul encourage? How can your prayer life become more aligned with this example of profound worship and passionate response?

2. This chapter reminds us that real worship-based prayer motivates deep confession of sin. Can you think of times when your confession was shallow and insincere? Do you have an idea as to why it was this way? Do you think a more powerful encounter of worship might have changed your approach? Explain.

3. Review the testimony of the work of prayer the Lord is doing in Quebec. What stands out to you as the most significant part of the story? How can you apply this example to your life or your local church?

Chapter 13: Pray This, Not That

1. In his practical teachings found in Matthew 6:5–13, Jesus was essentially saying, "Pray this, not that." After reading this chapter, what approach in your prayer life could you reevaluate in order to comply with Jesus' teachings in this passage?

2. This chapter talks about motivational mistakes. Which one of these challenges you? Take a moment to ask the Lord to search your heart and give you the grace to refine your motivation in prayer.

3. Review the bullet points that summarize what we should and should not do in prayer. Which of these ideas challenge

you to make adjustments in your current approach to prayer? What needs to change in order to advance your prayer experience? Commit these changes to the Lord today.

Chapter 14: Transforming Prayer for Dummies

1. What pattern of prayer have you used in the past? Was it effective? Would you share it with others? What value do you find in the 4/4 pattern presented in this chapter?

2. Why did Jesus want us to begin our prayers with a focus on God and His character rather than our own needs? Did any of the quotes or ideas from this chapter strengthen your resolve to begin with a worship-based focus? Explain.

3. Reread the section about readiness for the spiritual battle. Has this focus been a regular part of your prayer life? Why do you think Jesus made it a core component in prayer? How will you incorporate this into your prayer life?

Chapter 15: This Is How We Do It

1. In this chapter we see that a "request-based" approach can run out of steam after a short time. Have you ever experienced this? What happened? How did you feel?

2. After reading this chapter, take time to practice one of the examples. Whether on your own or with others, read the passage and select one of the sample prayers under each part of the 4/4 pattern. Ask the Holy Spirit to use His Word to inspire your heart and mind as you do this.

3. Review the four questions that align with the 4/4 pattern. Now turn to Psalm 23 and use this pattern to pray. Again, ask the Holy Spirit to guide and inspire your heart as you seek to experience this Scripture-fed, Spirit-led, worship-based approach to prayer.

Chapter 16: Coming Out of the Prayer Closet

1. Review the sense of community the early church enjoyed in prayer. Do you think this contributed to their spiritual unity and power? Is their pattern similar to that of your own church? How is it different? What can you do to see some positive change?

2. Evaluate Gene Getz's statement. What parts do you agree with? Do you disagree in any way? How can you be a positive contributor to an effort to experience greater community in prayer and to counteract a spirit of individualism?

3. In reviewing this chapter, do you agree that the devil works diligently to keep Christians from praying together? Can you effectively counter his efforts in your own church? What truths from this chapter will equip you to do so?

Chapter 17: Your Role in Organic Revival

1. Consider the news headlines that open this chapter. As you think of your own community, what headline would you love to see in the local newspaper that would show evidence of a revival of God's people? With this goal in mind, ask the Lord for faith to believe in His power and grace to see change in your community.

2. As you review Acts 6:1–7, what aspect of the story challenges your heart? What can you do to contribute in a more positive way to seeing this kind of supernatural work of the gospel occur in your church or community?

3. Byron Paulus says, "The biggest billboard for revival is a changed life." As you complete this book, think of specific ways in which you can be that billboard. Pray for the transformation in your life that will make it so. Trust the living Christ to work in and through you to spark a work of revival in your home, church, and community for His glory.

Notes

1. A. B. Simpson, from the booklet *Himself* (Camp Hill, PA: Christian Publications, Inc., 1885, 1990).

INTRODUCTION: The Road to Real Change

1. George Barna, *Revolution* (Carol Stream, IL: Tyndale House, 2005), 31–32.

CHAPTER 1: Beyond a "Grocery List" of Needs

1. D. A. Carson, *A Call to Spiritual Reformation* (Grand Rapids: Baker Academic, 1992), 182.

2. J. Oswald Sanders, *Prayer Power Unlimited* (Chicago: Moody Press, 1977), 11.

3. I first told Lori's story in *Fresh Encounters* (Colorado Springs: NavPress, 2004).

CHAPTER 2: The Potential for Transformation

1. Pastor Cymbala and I have recently launched a national cross-denominational pastors' network called The 6:4 Fellowship—focused on the priorities of Acts 6:4. For more information, go to *www.64fellowship.com*.

CHAPTER 3: What Is Blocking the Breakthrough?

1. "Study shows only 16 percent of Protestant ministers are very satisfied with their personal prayer lives," Grey Matter Research, *www.greymatterresearch.com/index_files/Prayer.htm*.

2. J. Oswald Sanders, *Spiritual Leadership* (Chicago: Moody Press, 1994), 85.

3. J. Oswald Sanders, *Prayer Power Unlimited* (Chicago: Moody Press, 1997), 10.

4. Daniel Henderson, *PRAYzing!* (Colorado Springs: NavPress, 2004).

5. D. A. Carson, *A Call to Spiritual Reformation* (Grand Rapids: Baker Academic, 1992), 35.

CHAPTER 4: Face Time!

1. *Pediatrics Journal*, The American Academy of Pediatrics (Elk Grove Village, IL: September 1978), Vol. 62, No. 3, 40.

2. *www.forbes.com/forbesinsights/Business_Meetings_FaceToFace/index.html.*

CHAPTER 5: Glowin' Moses and a Transformed You

1. *www.britannica.com/EBchecked/topic/66087/bioluminescence.*

2. Matt Redman, *The Unquenchable Worshipper* (Ventura, CA: Regal, 2001), 62.

3. The epistle known to us as 2 Corinthians was prompted by Paul's need to defend his own authority and authenticity in light of false teachers that had infiltrated the Corinthian church. In an effort to make themselves look better, these self-aggrandizing traitors to truth did everything they could to defame Paul. They apparently demeaned everything from his appearance to his preaching to his personal credibility as a leader.

   Second Corinthians is Paul's most transparent and heartfelt letter. He loved this church in spite of their fumbling faith. Their relationship with Paul, doctrinal integrity, and fidelity to Christ were at stake. Without any sense of self-promotion, Paul "goes for the jugular" in describing the nature of real ministry and the source of supernatural power and impact. He had to win their hearts and point their minds back to Christ. He ultimately notes that his credibility as a minister of the gospel is rooted in the transformed lives he left behind in Corinth. This fruit could only be credited to the power and sufficiency of Christ.

4. "Oh, that will be glory for me, glory for me, glory for me, when by His grace I shall look on His face, that will be glory, be glory for me." From the hymn, "Oh, That Will Be Glory" by Charles Gabriel, published 1900. Public domain.

5. Calvin Miller, *Into the Depths of God* (Minneapolis: Bethany House, 2000), 120.

CHAPTER 6: The Case of the Missing Prayer List

1. *http://searchsoftwarequality.techtarget.com/sDefinition/0,sid92_gci498678,00.html.*

2. Ibid.

3. For more information about this prayer tool, visit *www.pray2959.com.*

4. Perhaps the most extensive "prayer list" is found in 1 Timothy 2:1–5, where Paul writes, "Therefore I exhort first of all that supplications, prayers, intercessions, and giving of thanks be made for all men, for kings and

all who are in authority, that we may lead a quiet and peaceable life in all godliness and reverence. For this is good and acceptable in the sight of God our Savior, who desires all men to be saved and to come to the knowledge of the truth." The emphasis here is a variety of prayer expressions focused on societal leadership and a believer's responsibility to live in ways that adorn the gospel, with an ultimate goal of evangelism.

CHAPTER 7: All Prayer Requests Are Not Created Equal

1. A. W. Tozer, "Beware the File-Card Mentality," from the book *Of God and Men* (Harrisburg, PA: Christian Publications, 1960), 70–71.

2. Ibid., 71.

3. Ibid., 72.

4. John Franklin, *And the Place Was Shaken—How to Lead a Powerful Prayer Meeting* (Nashville: Broadman and Holman, 2005), 33–34.

5. D. A. Carson, *A Call to Spiritual Reformation* (Grand Rapids: Baker Academic, 1992), 96–97.

CHAPTER 8: Go for the Glory!

1. John Piper, *The Dangerous Duty of Delight* (Sisters, OR: Multnomah, 2001), 17.

2. John Piper sermon, "Prayer: The Power of Christian Hedonism," October 23, 1983, *www.desiringgod.org*.

3. Jonathan Edwards, *Dissertation Concerning the End for Which God Created the World,* in *The Works of Jonathan Edwards*, Vol. 8, ed., Paul Ramsey (New Haven, CT: Yale University Press, 1989), 526.

4. Daniel Henderson, with Patricia Roberts, *The Seven Most Important Questions You'll Ever Answer* (Forest, VA: Strategic Renewal, 1998), 15.

5. *http://bobrawleigh.org/bobsstory.html*.

CHAPTER 9: How Abiding Guides Our Asking

1. Calvin Miller, *The Path to Celtic Prayer* (Downers Grove, IL: InterVarsity Press, 2007), 57.

2. Charles Spurgeon, as cited in *A 12-Month Guide to Better Prayer* (Uhrichsville, OH: Barbour Publishing, 2009), 38.

3. Taken from a recent e-mail but based on Bud McCord's excellent book *The Satisfying Life, www.thesatisfyinglife.com*.

4. John Piper sermon, "Ask Whatever You Wish," January 10, 1993, *www.desiringgod.org*.

5. A. W. Pink, *Exposition of the Gospel of John* (Grand Rapids: Zondervan, 1975), 827.

6. George Muller, *Autobiography of George Muller* (Denton, TX: Westminster Literature Resources, 2003), 153.

7. Ibid., 154.

8. John Piper sermon, "How to Pray for a Desolate Church," January 5, 1992, *www.desiringgod.org*.

9. A. W. Pink, 825.

10. Andrew Murray, *With Christ in the School of Prayer* (Old Tappan, NJ: Revell, 1953), 122.

11. Ibid., 125.

12. Ibid.

13. John Stott, *Christ the Liberator* (Downers Grove, IL: InterVarsity Press, 1971), 57.

CHAPTER 10: How His Spirit Ignites Our Supplication

1. For information about the Barricks' story, including testimonies, videos, and booking details, visit *www.knowingjesusministries.net*.

2. Francis Chan, *Forgotten God* (Colorado Springs: David C. Cook, 2009), 15.

3. Ibid., 16.

4. John Calvin, *Institutes of the Christian Religion*, trans., Henry Beveridge, Vol. 1 (Grand Rapids: Eerdmans, 1964), 72.

5. William Law, *The Power of the Spirit* (Fort Washington, PA: Christian Literature Crusade, 1971), 19.

6. Kenneth S. Wuest, *Ephesians and Colossians in the Greek New Testament* (Grand Rapids: Eerdmans, 1953), 145.

7. John Piper sermon, "Learning to Pray in the Spirit and the Word"—Part 2, January 7, 2001, *www.desiringgod.org*.

8. D. M. M'Intyre, *In His Likeness* (London: Marshall, Morgan & Scott, n.d.), 28.

9. J. Oswald Sanders, *Prayer Power Unlimited* (Chicago: Moody Press, 1977), 62.

CHAPTER 11: How His Name Corrects Our Nonsense

1. Helen H. Lemmel, "Turn Your Eyes Upon Jesus," 1922. Public domain.

2. As early as Genesis, He is "God Most High" or *El Elyon* (Genesis 14:22), "the God-Who-Sees" (Genesis 16:13), "Almighty God" (Genesis 17:1), "the Eternal God" (Genesis 21:33 NIV), "The-Lord-Will-Provide" (Genesis 22:14), and "*El Elohe* [God of] Israel" (Genesis 33:20). The two essential and personal names of God in the Hebrew Scriptures are *Elohim* (used early in Genesis) and *Jehovah* (Yahweh), first revealed to Moses at the burning bush in Exodus 3; Yahweh is the eternal, self-existent "I AM," who brings all things into being and is the covenant-keeping Mighty God.

3. Edmund P. Clowney, *A Biblical Theology of Prayer,* from the book *Teach Us to Pray,* edited by D. A. Carson (Grand Rapids: Baker, 1990), 139.

4. Samuel Chadwick, *The Path of Prayer* (London: Hodder & Stoughton, 1936), 52.

5. W. Bingham Hunter, *The God Who Hears* (Downers Grove, IL: Inter-Varsity Press, 1986), 198.

6. Ibid., 198.

7. Randal Roberts, *Praying in the Name of Jesus*, from the book *Giving Ourselves to Prayer* (Terre Haute, IN: PrayerShop Publishing, 2008), 47.

8. John MacArthur, *Philippians* (Chicago: Moody Publishers, 2001), 14.

CHAPTER 12: How Revelation Motivates Our Response

1. As told by F. F. Bruce, *The Epistle of Paul to the Romans* (Grand Rapids: Eerdmans, 1963), 58–60.

2. Quoted by J. Sidlow Baxter, *Explore the Book* (Grand Rapids: Zondervan, 1960), Vol. 6, 66.

3. A. W. Tozer, *The Pursuit of God* (Camp Hill, PA: Christian Publications, 1982), 91.

4. John Piper sermon, "Prayer: The Work of Missions," July 29, 1988, *www.desiringgod.org*.

5. Patrick Johnstone and Jason Mandryk, *Operation World* (Pasadena, CA: Gabriel Resources, 2005), 145.

6. For more information about this wonderful ministry, see *www.sembeq.qc.ca/site/sembeq/*.

CHAPTER 13: Pray This, Not That

1. John MacArthur, *Jesus' Pattern of Prayer* (Chicago: Moody Press, 1981), 9.

2. Cited in *My Path of Prayer*, ed. David Hanes (Worthington, West Sussex: Henry E. Walter, 1981), 57.

CHAPTER 14: Transforming Prayer for Dummies

1. John MacArthur, *Jesus' Pattern of Prayer* (Chicago: Moody Press, 1981), 10.

2. Ibid., 20.

3. I highly recommend several books on the Lord's Prayer, including: *On Earth as It Is in Heaven* by Warren Wiersbe (Baker); *Jesus' Pattern of Prayer* by John MacArthur (Moody); and *Living Prayer* by Dennis Fuqua (*www.livingprayer.net*).

4. Derek Thomas, *Praying the Saviour's Way* (Ross-shire, Scotland: Christian Focus Publications, 2002), 43.

5. A. W. Tozer, *The Knowledge of the Holy* (San Francisco: Harper San Francisco, 1992), 1.

6. Robert Law, *The Tests of Life* (Edinburgh: T & T Clark, 1909), 304.

7. Warren Wiersbe, *On Earth as It Is in Heaven* (Grand Rapids: Baker, 2010), 68.
8. Ibid., 91.

CHAPTER 15: This Is How We Do It
1. More information about *The 29:59 Plan* is available at *www.pray2959.com*.

CHAPTER 16: Coming Out of the Prayer Closet
1. Gene Getz, *Praying for One Another* (Wheaton, IL: Victor Books, 1983), 11.
2. Randy Frazee, *The Connecting Church* (Grand Rapids: Zondervan, 2001), 42.
3. Ibid., 85.
4. Michael Griffiths, *God's Forgetful Pilgrims* (Grand Rapids: Eerdmans, 1978), 24.
5. A few years ago, my wife and I were touring Scotland, enjoying the many castles and palaces of my historic motherland. While visiting the Palace of Holyroodhouse, in Edinburgh, we noticed a portion of the historic royal residence identified as the Queen's Closet and the King's Closet. We anticipated a tidy collection of royal robes, fancy shoes, and other exquisite clothing accessories. What we discovered was quite surprising. When this palace was built by King James VI (the same one who authorized the 1611 translation of the Bible into English), a "closet" was not a little storage area for the safekeeping of clothes (as we understand it today). Rather, it was a special meeting room. To be called to the King's Closet in that day was a rare privilege, indicating you were part of an inner circle of close acquaintances or special guests.
6. To join our list of devotional recipients, go to *www.strategicrenewal.com*.
7. Daniel Henderson, *Keeping Perspective—Truths that Shape a Life of Influence* (Forest, VA: Strategic Renewal, 2010).

CHAPTER 17: Your Role in Organic Revival
1. John MacArthur, *The MacArthur Study Bible* (Nashville: Thomas Nelson, 2006), 1610.
2. J. Edwin Orr, *The Role of Prayer in Spiritual Awakening*—DVD (Orlando: Campus Crusade for Christ, 1976).
3. Ibid.; also *The Power of Extraordinary Prayer* by Robert O. Bakke (Wheaton, IL: Crossway, 2000).
4. This is the vision of The 6:4 Fellowship. For more information, go to *www.64fellowship.com*.

Acknowledgments

My thanks to:

Rosemary, my best friend for almost thirty years. I am grateful for your grace and patience every time I face a book deadline and enter my "writing world," usually to the neglect of other priorities. I am blessed by your gracious endurance and support.

Justin, Jordan, and Heather, for loving and praying for your dad. Your lives of faithful service to Christ continue to inspire me with joy as my children walk in truth. Justin, thank you, especially, for carrying the load in our offices as I took extra time to write.

Christa and Danyelle, for being such gracious "daughters-in-love," who have brought a fresh fragrance of Christ into the environment of our family.

Kyle Duncan, for your friendship and gracious confidence in the message the Lord has put in my heart. It is a privilege to be part of the Bethany House family.

Bill and Anna Lockrem and Stacy and Shannon Barr, for your patient editing of the rough draft of this book.

Sandi Selland, for editing the testimonies as a gracious expression of your own passion for worship-based prayer.

To the board of Strategic Renewal, for giving me the freedom to write and represent our vision through these books.

My prayer partners around the nation: Great is your reward in heaven. Only eternity will reveal the value of your investment in my ministry and in the lives that will be blessed by this book.